A HISTORY OF CRIMINAL TUDOR ENGLAND

It was a litigious century, and few there were who never rubbed shoulders with the officers of the law.

G.R. Elton

Duke: *We have strict statutes and most biting laws,*
The needful bits and curbs to headstrong jades
Which for these fourteen years we have let slip;
Even like an o'er-grown lion in a cave
That goes not out to prey ...

Shakespeare, *Measure for Measure*

For Amy Jordan, who has always helped and encouraged me

A HISTORY OF CRIMINAL TUDOR ENGLAND

STEPHEN WADE

First published in Great Britain in 2026 by
PEN AND SWORD TRUE CRIME
An imprint of
Pen & Sword Books Limited
Yorkshire – Philadelphia

ISBN 978 1 03619 526 7

A CIP catalogue record for this book is available from the British Library.

Typeset in Times New Roman 12/16 by SJmagic DESIGN SERVICES, India.
Printed and bound in the UK by CPI Group (UK) Ltd.

The Publisher's authorised representative in the EU for product safety is Authorised Rep Compliance Ltd., Ground Floor, 71 Lower Baggot Street, Dublin D02 P593, Ireland.
www.arccompliance.com

For a complete list of Pen & Sword titles please contact
PEN & SWORD BOOKS LIMITED
George House, Units 12 & 13, Beevor Street, Off Pontefract Road,
Barnsley, South Yorkshire, S71 1HN, England
E-mail: enquiries@pen-and-sword.co.uk
Website: www.pen-and-sword.co.uk

or

PEN AND SWORD BOOKS
1950 Lawrence Rd, Havertown, PA 19083, USA
E-mail: uspen-and-sword@casematepublishers.com
Website: www.penandswordbooks.com

Contents

Introduction

This is a court of law, young man, not a court of justice.
Oliver Wendell Holmes

The world around us as we contemplate the Tudor dynasty (1485–1603) might seem anarchic, constantly at war and packed with injustice and inequalities, but what strikes the modern reader studying the years following the accession of Henry VIII through to the death of Elizabeth I have been presented by the media and literature as brutal and inhuman. The images we repeatedly have before us when we think of Henry VIII and his six wives, or the reigns of the following sovereigns, are perhaps dominated by suffering and cruelty.

Television dramas, popular novels and films appear to depict a succession of political power which rules by terror; a series such as *Inside the Tower of London* (Channel 5) highlights the fact that visitors trail around that noble building to see the Crown Jewels, wonder at the huge White Tower, and then they want to know about the execution of Anne Boleyn. The world of Tudor crime and law holds a place in the popular imagination on a par with Nazi atrocity or the Spanish Inquisition. A rhyme among the popular clerihew doggerel of historical writing shows much of the attitudes:

Elizabeth the first
Was said to thirst
For Essex in bed
But remained unwed.

For the popular imagination, the Tudors represent the narratives of royal British history: these persist as distortions and exaggerations, but a mesmerising shimmer of regalia, gold and passions gathers around the facts that people generally like to fasten on. Arguably, it is the fascinating paradoxes of the age that form a basis of much of this. But the fact is that in the narrative of the Tudor monarchs the materials of popular genre narratives are all there, and plain to see: desire, ambition, vanity, cruelty, lies, betrayal and political strategy lie at the very core of the human stories. The literature of the century also adds to the complexity of the web of personal ambitions fastened tightly onto the story of a succession of rises and falls of the principal actors in the stories. Thomas More, author of a life of Richard III which played a key role in defining the monstrous villain of Shakespeare's play, also imagined a utopia in his book of that name; Niccolo Machiavelli wrote a book which in some ways defines many of the political attitudes of the age, with statements such as:

> Nothing wins a ruler respect like great military victories and a display of remarkable personal qualities. One example in our own times is Ferdinand of Aragon, the present King of Spain. One might almost describe him as a ruler new to power because from being a weak king he has become the most famous and honoured of Christendom, and when you look at his achievements you find they are all remarkable … At the beginning of his reign he launched an invasion of Granada, a campaign that laid the foundation of his power.

We are, then, to admire a ruler because he invades, conquers and subdues. Power is taken and is desirable and necessary. When Henry VIII, in the years before the 1530s, worked hard to become a sovereign to rival his counterparts in Europe, we may see this kind of ambition advertised for all to see. In 1520 he held the Field of the Cloth of Gold; this was a rich, showy event to display the wealth and talents of himself and Francis I of France, with a tournament at the centre of attractions. Henry invested in developing the British navy also, and in consolidating his status by building several palaces which he would visit up and down the land, with his court always on the move, hunting, feasting and what today we might call high-level networking.

There was a downside to all this Tudor land of popular myth and media, of course. In the reign of Henry VII there might have been the excitement of the encroachment into the Americas, but, as research done in 2025 confirms, Columbus brought syphilis to Europe. A report on research done by Dr Casey Kirkpatrick and others explains this: 'The new research, published in the journal *Nature* tips the scales in favour of the Columbian theory. It focuses on ancient human bones and teeth recovered from Mexico, Chile, Peru and Argentina which also appear to have what appear to be syphilitic lesions.' The widespread impact of this is observed in the spread of syphilis across Europe, where mercenary armies were constantly in use.

At the very centre of life was the church and worship, and again the growth of heritage industry, cultural narratives and dramatic tales of horrific deaths by martyrs and other victims, adds another layer of Tudor imagery in the popular imagination. Visitors to York, for instance, crowd into the medieval street known as The Shambles, and there they will see the home of Margaret Clitherow, a brave woman (now Saint Margaret) who died for her insistence on maintaining her faith against the brutal impositions of the regime of a Protestant power base; her story culminates in her being pressed to death, which was the punishment for those who would not enter a plea at trial; this entailed her being placed under heavy weight of wood and stone until she expired in agony.

The great historian, G.R. Elton, writing in 1960, wrote:

> The existing situation proved intense, because the laity feared, resented and despised much about the church, its

> officers, its courts and its wealth … A wide ramification of jurisdiction, a mixture of high claims and low deeds did not make for respect or love among the laity …

We need to enquire into the nation itself, as it was at the end of the divisive, often very brutal years of the Yorkist–Lancastrian conflicts. To understand the nature of the crime and the changes in law, the land itself has to be understood. The England at the beginning of the Tudor dynasty was described very informatively by S.T. Bindoff seventy years ago:

> The fifteenth-century retreat of arable before pasture, of crops before sheep, was a logical readjustment of the rural economy of the needs and capacities of a declining population. It had involved little hardship and provoked no resistance. But a population which was beginning to increase again had either to recover the lost acres for the plough or to work its reduced ploughlands more intensively … temporarily at least, land-surfeit gave place to land-hunger. It was no longer only sheep which competed among themselves, but men who competed with sheep …

The population of England at this time has been estimated at around 2.3 million in 1520, rising to almost 4 million in 1600. What strikes the student of the early years of Henry VII and his son Henry VIII is just how much major influences on belief and on the church and state still persisted. Shakespeare's father, John, a glove-maker of Stratford, would have been still quite sharply aware of the impact of Lollardy, the great phase of religious and spiritual dissent that took its name from John Wycliffe (1328–84). Lollard beliefs had several elements, but most challenging to orthodox Christianity would have been the rejection of the basic certainty that in transubstantiation in the mass, there was a real presence of Christ. They preferred the notion of 'consubstantiation' and the consequences could be horrendous; a certain William Sawtry had been burned for such opinions in 1401. They also had no belief in the baptism and confession acts as being needed for the soul's salvation.

This was a serious business. In 1395 parliament was petitioned and twelve 'Conclusions' were formulated and nailed to the door of Westminster Hall. One of the most significant of these was to be a central issue much later – that church professionals should not spend time and effort on political rather than spiritual matters.

Lollardy persisted. The story of Thomas Bilney proves this, as he was a scholar and churchman who was influenced by these notions, and he preached rather too often and too notably, so that he was dragged to the Tower, and was eventually convicted of heresy; at first he recanted and escaped his deadly fate, but later he was arrested, tried and then burnt at a place called Lollards' Pit at Norwich in August 1531.

John Shakespeare would have also been closer to the aftermath of the Wars of the Roses, and to the memory of events in what historian Barbara Tuchman has called 'the calamitous fourteenth century' which, as well as Lollardy, had the Black Death of 1348–49, starvation, foreign wars and increasing problems of the labouring poor. The latter issue resulted in the 1381 Peasants' Revolt. His son, William, would have been well aware of such earlier influences of attitudes around him as he developed into the London-based dramatist with his finger on the pulse of contemporary political and moral issues.

There was also another important factor in everyday life for the workers as well as for the manorial lords: preparation for the defence of the realm. With no standing army nor professional police, the stress was on weapons being available to people; Henry VIII in particular was keen on archery, even when the first versions of guns were around the place and being used in war. Men were supposed to have weapons at the ready and to know how to use them. The bill and the bow were the most common articles in use, but of course, gentlemen carried swords and daggers were also common.

In one local muster roll for 1522, where people and their arms were recorded in a general inventory, this is part of a listing:

> Individual value of land value of goods
> Edward Jakeman 10.00 80.00
> Richard Hamerton 2.00 1.00
> John Clerke (vicar) 19.00 20.00

In Henry VIII's time, there were repeated threats to the peace of his land from France and Scotland, for instance. In the case of Scotland, he had defeated the Scottish king James IV (who had married Henry's sister) at the Battle of Flodden in 1513, but the northern borders were always an area of fragility in terms of the measures taken for defence. Musters were held usually once or sometimes twice annually, and people were expected to attend. The exercise involved valuations of items owned, so it was a sort of minor *Domesday Book*, and as A.C. Chibnall has written, there were difficulties: 'Wolsey had helped to identify some of the loopholes. In an attempt to tighten up, people were given a year's notice to assess their wealth and worth. In March 1522, everyone was commanded to attend the muster where they had to declare on oath details of wealth, property and "harness" in case of war. These details were recorded, and the King's servants/inspectors employed to check that they were correct.'

Another factor stands out in Tudor life and beliefs, and it has a significant bearing on crime. This is the world of folk belief, superstition, magic and sorcery. If we had to select another standard image of the period as seen by modern media, it probably would be witchcraft. Witchcraft itself was related to religion, but the more widespread interest in everything related to occult and mystical practices was a constant part of Tudor life. Understanding this is not too hard; after all, in the 1920s Sir Arthur Conan Doyle believed in the Cottingley Fairies hoax, and even more informative regarding the need humans have for the illogicality of such things as reading palms and tea leaves is the 2025 report on fortune telling in France in *The Daily Telegraph.* In September of that year the report noted that in France the fortune telling industry is estimated to be worth €3 billion a year, and this is so in spite of the statement that: 'The French authorities … are under pressure to regulate it [the industry] after claims by the National Institute of Divinatory Arts that three quarters of the country's 100,000 fortune tellers are incompetent and dishonest.'

One could draw a further contrast with the Early Modern world in *The Telegraph* angle on the phenomenon: 'The French like to think of themselves as a bastion of rationality in an uncertain world, shaped by thinkers such as René Descartes, the 17th century mathematician.'

In the case of witchcraft, under Athelstan back in the mid-tenth century, murder by witchcraft was punishable by death, and by the thirteenth century it could be linked to heresy, as it entailed some kind of association with Satan. In the mid-Tudor period the Acts of 1542 and 1563 related to a definite predominance of a persecution campaign, and by 1604, with the ascent of James I (who was himself determined to stamp out witchcraft) there was more rigour behind investigations and punishments.

A general overview of factors involving social history will always influence the understanding of Tudor crime and justice when inspected through modern eyes. The reign of Henry VII between Bosworth and 1509 when his son took over and the term 'Henrician' we use today points directly at the Henry who dominates our views of this century, has a reputation of being fixed on financial and taxation themes. A general view of him notes his inexperience of government; but, of course, there were still remnants of dissent and open opposition. As one historian explains, 'The first challenge from Yorkist irreconcilables came in April 1486, was headed by Lord Lovell and the Hastings brothers … it was followed by the Simnel

Plot in 1487. Simnel claimed to be Edward, Earl of Warwick, despite the fact that Warwick was in the tower.' Shakespeare's famous words 'Uneasy lies the head that wears a crown' seems to apply well to Henry VII. On the credit side, his measures to avoid having to work with parliaments was achieved by taking what he could from any source to add to the crown funds.

The social history behind this, up to the accession of Henry VIII in 1509 meant, more than any other determining factor in ordinary life, that there was peace, in spite of the royal claimants' activities. As always happens through these years when it comes to consolidation of power and the essential accruing of finance, the law was used. When Henry VII came to power it is reckoned that income from crown lands were merely around £3,000; at his death, this had reached the figure of £300,000. This links to arguably the first murders at the hands of his son, Henry, because the two principal activists in dragging people to court in the Star Chamber (whose work we will describe later) were Richard Empson and Edmund Dudley. Their methods of increasing revenue led to general hatred, and sure enough, Henry VIII rubbed them out as he started the clean sweep behind his new regime.

There is one more feature of Tudor life, notably after the ascent of Elizabeth to the throne, which explains a massive paradox in our modern view of this era. This lies in the fact, evident in one of the richest and most exceptional periods in English literature and drama, that the same regime which fostered extreme and barbaric punishment was the same one that lay behind the patronage and encouragement of the highest art. At the base of this is something that the poet T.S. Eliot touched on in one of his influential literary essays, 'The Metaphysical Poets':

> Tennyson and Browning are poets, and they think; but they do not feel their thought as immediately as the odour of a rose. A thought to Donne was an experience; it modified his sensibility. When a poet's mind is perfectly

> equipped for its work, it is constantly amalgamating disparate experience; the ordinary man's experience is chaotic, irregular, fragmentary. The latter falls in love, or reads Spinoza, and these two experiences have nothing to do with each other … in the mind of the poet these experiences are always forming new wholes.

This is an opinion on the minuteness in creativity which comes from a deep and adventurous enquiry into human nature. But there was always the wider, philosophical view in this era also, and one of the clearest expressions of this sensitivity and richness of insight is in Hamlet's famous soliloquy about the human creature:

> What a piece of work is a man, how noble in reason, how infinite in faculties, in form and moving how express and admirable, in action how like and angel, in apprehension how like a god; the beauty of the world, the paragon of animals – and yet to me, what is this quintessence of dust? Man delights not me – nor woman neither …

Eliot's point is that the Tudor and Stuart period saw a special wealth of talent in the kind of thinking and feeling that a crucially important time in human thought and creativity brings. He sees this in the interior world of the creative mind. Shakespeare, in contrast, sees these insights when placed in a context of deeper philosophy, and reactions to the paradoxes of mankind. Nothing could be more relevant than these perceptions when it comes to understanding crime and law in this period. One reason for this is that an age under threats from both inside the individual (his and her spiritual life) and from outside in their political world (Spain's designs on their land, new rules and laws about worship and so on) will be an age in which there is instability. A word used in social science for this instability as it is expressed in the individual is anomie, coined by Émile Durkheim in the 1890s, and this will be discussed in the next chapter. It relates to a sense of being estranged from norms of social and ideological stability, and its links to crime and other varieties of transgression are obvious: it creates restlessness, doubt and fear.

When we see Tudor crime shown on stage in the plays of Shakespeare we have a similar presentation of crime in the society around our Bard of Avon. Serious crime is at the heart of the great tragedies and history plays; in *Othello* the play ends with the murder of Desdemona; in *Hamlet*, the king had killed his brother (Hamlet's father) and in *Macbeth* and *Julius Caesar* similarly, there are murders at the core of the stories. In his work of popular history of 1911, *Life in Shakespeare's England*, John Dover Wilson uses two plays to explain the lives and crimes of 'rogues and vagabonds' and Shakespeare's own insights into transgression and deviance find effective expression in his brilliant monologues in the mouths of countless villains.

Was the Tudor period as bad as it seems through the images of people burnt at the stake for witchcraft or for heresy? Was the period one of repeated repression and barbarity imposed on those who dissented from the norm of belief or who committed serious crime? The short answer is yes. There was a great deal of crime in that world, and it is helpful to summarise phases of historical development between the battle of Bosworth in 1485 in which Henry Tudor defeated Richard III and the Gunpowder Plot in 1604, just after the accession of James I (Sixth of Scotland).

This overview gives us an idea of the sheer scale of social change in this period of religious upheaval.

First, Henry VII, the first Tudor and victor of Bosworth, emerged after the end of the Wars of the Roses. The red rose of the Tudors was to be placed wherever the rulers fancied, and the reign of Henry VII had to be a period of resetting things after a century of internecine warfare across England.

Second, when Henry VIII took the throne in 1509, the land was about to experience the massive shock of the ascent of a monarch who was to transform everything, removing the Pope from direct power over a European Christendom which had defined identity and belief for millions.

After that, the effects of the European Reformation gradually percolated into thinkers, preachers and lawmakers. Practices of belief and worship switched identities as monarchs changed.

Finally, in the reign of Elizabeth I the threat from Spain led to the Armada; here was a threat to the crown and country that would have led to a fundamental, existential change in society. England survived.

The ordinary people who lived through these years must have felt as if the world was a dizzying, confusing place, with changing power bases and structures, as their once familiar world of mostly agricultural stability and village politics faded. The fundamentals of survival had always been, for a mostly farm- and manor-based society, wool, sheep, agrarian produce and the church in a world in which people knew their place and which limited their aspirations.

In between the progress of these great phases of change there had been particular events of immense importance for everyone, such as the arrival in America by John Cabot in 1497; the excommunication of Queen Elizabeth in 1579; Martin Luther's declaration against indulgences in 1517; Magellan's circumnavigation of the world in 1519, and in 1571 the Battle of Lepanto off Greece which crushed the Islamic navy.

Studying the nature and progress of everyday crime against this backdrop of great, transmuting history might seem like a diversion into something trivial, but that is far from the truth. When, in *Measure for Measure*, the bawd, Mistress Overdone, says, 'Thus, what with the war, what with the sweat, what with the gallows, and what with poverty, I am custom-shrunk,' she was referring to four significant impacts of the ordinary lives of the people. Along with war and crime and being poor came the ever-present threat of horrendous disease, such as the 'sweating sickness' known as 'the English disease', which assailed folk alongside more ailments familiar to us today such as the pestilential plague and the results of impure water and insanitary conditions.

Telling the criminal stories means opening up the real sinews of Tudor life: when societies experience transgression, we could argue that rare insight occurs into the actual sensual, emotional and desperate experience of the citizens of a society. If one has to characterise the nature of Tudor society and crime, there have to be different arenas of activity. The lives of the nobility were tightly bound up with life and court, and the courts always on the move; ambitious aristocrats and self-made men worked to step up into closer contact with the higher echelons of the court itself, and the foundations of much of this wealth and status were rooted in the notions of an individual rising by merit and strategy. Hence there were links to all kinds of crime around this element of life.

But for ordinary people, the workers and managers rather than the movers and shakers, there was hard work and church; life was ruled by the religious calendar and the seasons; there was money in wood and wool, and stability was essential. In the first years of the sixteenth century, under Henry VII and then his son until the 1530s, ordinary folk would know that there was a king, and he ruled by grace of God; there was the Pope in Rome, and he was head of the church; there were the basic economics of survival, and most pressing of all concerns was the need to put food on the table and have a roof over one's head. The man was the head of the family, and everyone drew their morality from the teachings of the church and the holy scriptures.

There were obvious disruptions and problems around the country, such as the increasing numbers of vagrants roaming around and often making trouble. They had strayed from their own parish, and the parish was a fundamental institution. Somewhere, wrapped around all this was the idea of the law, and as the years went on under the Tudors, courts proliferated and transgressions became not only frequent but complicated.

Looking into a time like the sixteenth century and hoping for some clarity about the impact of all this background on the life under scrutiny, the words of Keith Jeffrey come to mind – there is something of a special challenge in historical study: 'The mute strangeness of things and the unfathomability of lives past.' With this in mind, as the following is an account of crime and law, there will be narratives of death, but these will not always be suspicious deaths. Thanks to research by Craig Spence, who has studied bills of mortality, we know much more about Tudor deaths through accidents and lack of care. The studies reveal for instance a death under a weight of fallen food, drowning after riding on a wet sheep, mis-firing a gun, and being suffocated by a fish that fell on a man's mouth while he was sleeping.

But of course, my stories will feature a deal of murder and misfortune in an age of widespread robbery, assault and downright wilful killing. But, just to temper matters with a caveat, plenty of miscreants escaped the noose or the block. As Frederick Wilkinson recalled, in his account of the history of weaponry, this kind of thing happened:

> Despite Henry VIII's decree about the killing of the king's officers, the maximum penalty was not always given. In 1590 there was a case in which men wearing gauntlets and privy coats attacked four bailiffs to release their prisoner, and killed one with the thrust of a rapier. When put on trial and found guilty the villains were not given the death penalty as the statute ordained. In 17 cases of murder, seven were found guilty but claimed benefit of clergy and escaped with a branding; six were hanged.

The benefit of clergy was a method of escaping the noose by being able to recite the 'neck verse' from the Bible. The important section is: 'Have mercy upon me oh God, according to thy loving kindness.

According unto the multitude of thy tender mercies, blot out my transgression …'

This book has relied for its stories and people upon the vast mountain of legal records we have, notably the plea rolls, which have seven centuries of parchment and therefore have relied on 6 million sheep, together with tales from the criminal courts mainly from assizes and magistrates. But the great, recorded stories of history always have their spin-off sources, such as the fascination one might feel for the now sainted Nicholas Owen, a joiner from Oxford who built priest holes at a time described by Christopher Howse very vividly: 'By the end of 1586 only 130 of the 300 priests who had returned to England from seminaries abroad were still at liberty. Some died in prison, 33 had been martyred, 50 were in prison …' Owen, writes Howse, at Baddesley Clinton 'made hides for priests and Mass-gear and built escape routes'.

The bit players certainly have their place in the history of crime.

Chapter 1

A World of Courts and Gaols

Laws, like houses, lean on one another.
Edmund Burke

When one looks at different periods in history in order to try to understand the nature of crime and criminal law, the Tudor period strikes one as inordinately perplexing. After Henry VIII's transmutation from ambitious young monarch to moody, immoral despot and master of church and state, the ordinary citizen surely must have felt that any move made away from routine life and work was fraught with challenges, and many of these involved courts of law.

The important event in this ascendency of the king was the 1534 Act of Supremacy, its central statement being 'The King's Majesty justly and rightfully is and ought to be the Supreme Head of the Church of England.' As the historians J.J. Bagley and P.B. Rowley put it, the Act '… set aside the centuries-old concept of ecclesiastical and temporal administrations sharing power as twin authorities and established in England the Erastian church which has been so prominent a feature of the country ever since'. 'Erastian' meaning the placing of the church below the state, after Thomas Erastus (1524–83).

The actual words in the Act that define precisely the new power are these:

> Be it enacted by authority of this present parliament that the King our Sovereign Lord, his heirs and successors kings of

> this realm, shall be taken, accepted and reputed the only Supreme Head in earth of the Church of England called *Anglicana Ecclesia*, and shall have and enjoy annexed and united to the imperial crown of this realm as well as the style and title thereof, as all honours, dignitaries, pre-eminences, jurisdictions, privileges, authorities, immunities, profits and commodities to the said dignity of Supreme Head …

These are the words defining absolute power, reaching for the first time to two important events of immediate influence on the subjects of this new king with his fresh, revolutionary status: his ability to seize wealth and the necessity of some kind of opposition. Both these things happened very soon after this Act, and both determined what was to follow in terms of the use and abuse of this autocrat's adoption of the role of absolute Commander in Chief of everything.

The ordinary citizen was to find that breaking the law would lead not only to an appearance in court, but very likely some time behind bars, and a prison sentence was in many cases a death sentence. But as always in a state run on measures of rich and poor, in favour and out of favour, privilege and extreme poverty, all kinds of new offences were to arise. The great legal historian F.W. Maitland explained how far the king's power could go, and this is in the nature of what became royal 'proclamations' both in Henry's time and in the reign of his daughter Elizabeth:

> It certainly seems to have been the common opinion that the king had a certain ordaining power … Henry VIII obtained from parliament a Statute giving to his proclamations issued with the consent of the majority of his council the force of statute law … Elizabeth, we find, freely issues proclamations: thus Anabaptists are banished from the realm, Irishmen are commanded to depart into Ireland, the exportation of corn, money and

> various commodities are prohibited. A proclamation in 1580 forbids the erection of houses within three miles of London, under pain of imprisonment …

What was happening to criminal law was a clash of fundamental notions of what the law of the land was, what was the nature and power of common law, and who would control the courts. As matters stood in the 1530s, affairs of behaviour relating to anything church related were dealt with in the church courts; the magistracy across the land handled everything of local context from nuisances in the highway to assaults and murder, and then the judges on the assize circuits tried serious crime in their task of emptying the gaols. The culprits in the Quarter Sessions would be passed on to the assizes, after a wait in gaol, and the magistrates took the bulk of criminal work. But the issues the reader senses when looking at these years is the sheer wayward journey to create a distance between the ideas of the common law and the urgent needs of the new autocracy.

We can see the results of this sweeping away of common law thinking in an important case in legal history, Semayne's Case of 1604. But first, two fundamental concepts need to be explained. The first is 'the law of the land' and this is in Magna Carta (1215): 'No man shall be deprived but by *legem terrae*, the law of the land.' This reaches back to the years of the first Saxon law codes and the operation of everyday law in the small units of settlement, the hundreds and wapontakes, when the local leader gave and took advice regarding offences on their patch. The second is the common law. The great Tudor/Stuart jurist Sir Edward Coke wrote his legal classic, *Reports*, in order to mix a range of legal opinion on typical cases across the land, and he always included the definition of common law that is generally accepted: 'That is, by common law, statute law or custom of England … by the due course and process of law.' This statement includes the kind of lawmaking and court thinking Coke would have liked, and Semayne's Case shows this integration of thinking, using different bases of judgement.

The case came right at the beginning of the Stuarts, with James I, and it is especially interesting to look at before we consider crime from the standpoint of the early years of Henry VIII, almost eighty years previously.

The case is based on the joint tenants of a Blackfriars property, Richard Gresham and George Berisford. The latter was in debt to a certain Peter Semayne, and when Berisford died, he had property in the building which the creditor wanted to take in payment of monies owed to him. To do this, he had to enter the Blackfriars property, of course. Semayne acquired a civil writ to take this material, and the local sheriff intended to force his way into the house, but Semayne overrode this and he took an action against Gresham.

The court had to decide on the event of breaking and entering. Three justices thought that the sheriff could force an entry, and two others decided the opposite. Matters closed down in an impasse, until James was enthroned and the Court of Kings Bench sat again to consider Semayne and Gresham's confrontation. The verdict was in favour of Gresham, largely because it was seen as no felony for a citizen to defend his house *in extremis*, and that a sheriff could only force entry in specific conditions, such as a door being open to him.

This is where the importance of Coke and the common law enter the scene. Coke found a 1275 statute that made a common law precedent. The result of Semayne's case was our cliché that 'an Englishman's home is his castle'. But we can see, in the United States fourth amendment, the modern stipulations for America, in the words, 'No warrants will be issued without probable cause … warrants must specifically describe the place to be searched and the people or things to be seized.' As I write this in 2025, President Donald Trump's ICE corps surely do not follow this procedure as they search for illegal immigrants.

Back in the 1530s, with the new regime of Henry VIII – now 'Defender of the Faith' – in place, the courts were going to be busy, because by *c.*1540 the new leader had put in place the dissolution of the monasteries, and he and his proclamations had an army of restless people against them, in what became known as the Pilgrimage of Grace. But before we look at that, the power base in the new structure needs to be looked at. The sovereign and his courts, the organs of function for the justice system, were organised to cater for subjects of all classes, from aristocrats at the top to everyday workers or restless poor at the bottom.

At the core of all this system was the king's Privy Council. This was a body composed of special advisors; its work covered mainly matters of security, religion and military business, and was to supervise the working of justice. It had the power to decide on matters of national importance, but the monarch could exercise veto, and could also remove members, as Elizabeth did in 1597.

After the troubles of the 1530s, the Council of the North was established at York, and a journal written in the 1890s gives a neat summary of its reason for existence:

> It was vested with various powers of oyer and terminer [listen and act from decision] with jurisdiction over the counties of York, Durham, Hull and Newcastle, as being particularly prone to murmur and rebel against the royal authority. The Council became a sort of Star Chamber of the North, governing the counties under its sway with great tyranny and oppression, from which there was no appeal, so much, as Macaulay says, 'as to render the Great Charter a dead letter in the North'.

Through Tudor times, the list of Lord Presidents of the Council shows that the nation's leaders were there to run things. These included Thomas Howard, 3rd Duke of Norfolk, Francis Talbot, Earl of Shrewsbury, Henry Hastings and Thomas Cecil, 2nd Baron Burghley.

The Star Chamber, the Exchequer and the King's Bench were at the head of the courts, and are classed as superior courts; these were followed by the church or ecclesiastic courts, with the Archbishop of Canterbury's Court of Arches in the lead; then the diocesan courts; finally, there were the state courts with the magistracy in charge – the Quarter Sessions at which every category of offence was first heard.

The Quarter Sessions courts were always the workhorse of the criminal justice system throughout British history. They began in 1361, and they handled every kind of offence and local tribulation that came their way. They were the domain of the justices of the peace (magistrates) and met, as the name suggests, four times a year. Before the justices came concerns relating to drunkenness, pub brawls, arguments over land, nuisances on the highway, problems with beggars, licensing of beer houses, provision of constables, maintenance of bridges and other affairs, the topics changing as the years passed and society had new laws and fresh social problems. All the justices of the county generally sat on the bench at Quarter Sessions.

It was in the Tudor period that the justices really found their workload accelerating: a succession of legislative measures to deal with the increasing problems of vagrants, wanderers from other parishes and disabled soldiers, and also of affairs relating to apprentices and workmen, street crime and the regulation of all local matters pertaining to the social order. The magistrates were first created as a fresh form of the previous 'Keeper of the Peace' and it is no accident that they appeared and were more clearly defined at a time of massive social crisis. The Black Death of 1348 and the horrendous years of famine previous to that, along with other epidemics and social revolt, made the year of 1361 one of the most significant in British legal history. It saw an Act that set up Quarter Sessions the next year. The immediate context was one of the widespread threat of violence and roving gangs across the land.

Quarter Sessions dealt with capital offences until the 1660s and from that time there was also an increasing number of petty sessions, hearings often dealing with many of the matters the Quarter Sessions normally handled. The everyday offences before the magistrates were misdemeanours, crimes that could be tried without a jury. Of course, they were the place where the first appearance of a person arrested for a felony would appear too, the cases being handed on to the Assize hearing that came up next on the calendar.

In the nineteenth century, many local offences were dealt with by police courts, which were yet another form of petty session, but the Quarter Sessions went on, the centre of the great law machine in the heart of the social upheavals of the Industrial Revolution. Massive threats of riot and disorder were everywhere in the first three decades of that century, and Luddites, 'Captain Swing' rural crime and the Chartist movement added to the burden of the justices.

No End of Business

The justices had a massive amount of responsibility before them and they had to deal with several issues related to non-judicial duties as well as the criminal cases needing due process of law.

If we look at how trials at Quarter Sessions were conducted, there was generally a sequence of actions and topics. This organisation reflected the varied business of the court. First there would be *presentments* applied to all the waiting accused persons. These are statements of the alleged offences, so in turn these would appear to be charged. If the offence was a misdemeanour, this would be typical of what happened:

First, the Accused

'John Holmes of Keighley, blacksmith, for assaulting there on 13th March and maltreating John Greene, clerk. Witn. Ja. Ibbetson …' (Puts himself not guilty at Skipton, 18 July 1638)

His case had progressed to the Quarter Sessions from a hearing at petty sessions.

Then Appeals and Supervisions

This could include assessments of property, highway maintenance fines, repairs of bridges, issues relating to parish constables, financial accounts of various people in office, appeals against assessments, and until the Municipal Corporations Act of 1835, other business would include supervising boards of health, Poor Law unions and town councils. The non-judicial duties retained after that were mainly of licensing premises, arbitrating in master and servant disputes, supervising county rates, the sale of coals, bread and flour regulations and ensuring that friendly societies and trade unions (in the latter case with adaptations as such unions became legal). This may be most clearly seen at times of peril and threat towards the authorities, for instance during the Luddite violence around 1811–12 or the Chartists' agitations of the 1830s and 1840s. Equally, in the Tudor period and through to the 1834 Poor Law reforms, there would be issues such as vagrancy and social responsibility at this point.

A typical local session records a long list of crimes, and most were felonies, and so one possible punishment was death. Reading the account today, there is a deep sense of foreboding in the wording; sixteen men and two women were 'Put for good or ill upon the country, whereupon a jury was called'. We can imagine them all lined up before the twelve good men and true, waiting for their fate. The report goes on:

> … they were led to the bar by the sheriff and asked what they could say for themselves why they should not have judgement of death according to the law for the felonies aforesaid whereof they were convicted. They severally said that they were clerks and prayed for benefit of clergy to be granted them.

The neck verse, as explained in my introduction, was originally intended to give clergy an exemption from the criminal law process. An old verse explains:

If a clerk had been taken
For stealing of bacon,
For burglary, murder or rape.
If he could but rehearse
(well prompt) his neck verse,
He never could fail to escape.

But the unhappy line of men and women in the court, although they had learned the words well, had further pain to come. By a statute of Henry VII they had to be branded: each was burned in his left hand, according to the statute. The old statute said: 'every person so convicted of murder, be marked with an M upon the brawn of the left thumb, and if he be convicted for any other felony the same person to be marked with a T in the same place upon the thumb, and these marks to be made by a gaoler openly in court before the judge.' There were screams of agony that day in the courtroom.

Bertram Osborne, in his detailed study of the magistracy, stresses an important element in the organisation of the justices across the shires:

> From at least the time of Henry VII it was the practice to include in the Commission of the Peace the names of certain high officers of state and gentlemen of the royal household. Sometimes a member of the royal family itself would be included. Thus, the Archbishop of Canterbury, often a prominent member of the privy council, figured as a justice for a number of counties in company with noblemen or others who held such offices as Lord Chamberlain or Master of the Horse.

The ecclesiastical courts were close to everyone, as virtually every member of society and subject of the king went to church. In fact, not going to church was a crime under the new Protestant regime onwards. The topic of sin has to enter the stage here, as of course, Tudor Britain was still a land with the established views of life and death held by medieval Christendom. That means that heaven and hell were real to them. There was original sin and there were sins committed in the life on Earth, and these required absolution and atonement. Consequently the church courts dealt with and punished mainly matrimonial matters, heterosexual promiscuity, breakers of the Sabbath, regulation of the priesthood and other topics relating to interpersonal behaviour. These courts were in the hands of the clergy, and the archdeacon and bishops had their own.

A typical example of church court cases was that of an affray in Islington, and it had its roots in a feud. In winter, 1566 a sound was heard by a local man of 'chiding in the street'. A certain Margaret James was upset because another woman was annoying her by glaring at her. The offender was Elizabeth North, and Margaret had been heard calling her 'an arrant whore'. There was a man involved in fornication with Margaret and she had been subjected to one of the worst ordeals possible at that time – being called a whore in front of the church congregation. That was punishment enough, and the court knew it.

But the bishops across the land had always had their own gallows, and this tells us immediately just how much power they had. York Minster had its own prison during the Early Modern and medieval times, and acknowledgement of this power adds another weight to Henry VIII's desire to run things in his own land without having to counteract the church powers.

Then, above and beyond all this there were the assizes. These handled the serious crimes across all the shires, led by two or more judges acting on crown commission. They were to operate on circuits and deal with both civil and criminal offences. Since the twelfth century they had controlled *oyer* and *terminer*, as mentioned above; until the 1971 establishment of crown courts, these were the places of trial for the notorious serious crimes throughout British history.

Here, the subject of gaols becomes important. The assize trials cleared the gaols, where offenders had been waiting since their first committal after a session in a lower court. Notoriously, the county gaols were places where many were likely to die, mostly from typhus, the 'gaol fever'; there were many abuses in the penal system, and not until the late eighteenth century was there any proper inspection. The prisons also housed debtors, separated in their own wing or hall. It was also in this time that the houses of correction, or bridewells, were established, and this was based on the idea that prisoners in gaol for minor offences, particularly vagrancy, should work when locked up. This will be relevant again when we consider the problems of the homeless poor drifters who engaged in petty crime. The small gaols, or compters, also catered for minor offences, usually run by sheriffs, as was the Poultry Compter in Cheapside in the Tudor age.

Those convicted of serious felony were in for a hard death, and through the sixteenth century, treason was often on the indictment. This meant the condemned being hanged, drawn and quartered, as was a typical case in Lincoln. Thomas Sprott and Thomas Hunt are now both 'venerable' in the Catholic Church. This means that they have reached the first of the three degrees of canonisation, and so may eventually be saints. They suffered horribly for their beliefs, and were hanged, drawn and quartered at Lincoln on 11 July 1600.

Sprott was born at Skelsmergh, Kendal in Westmorland, and was ordained a priest in Douai at the English College in 1596. He was soon sent on a mission and on 8 November 1598 he signed a letter to the Pope, supporting the archpriest in England – a major Catholic figure whose presence of course, would be anathema to the queen. That was signing his own death warrant.

Hunt, who was from Norfolk, had been a student at the English College in Seville and been ordained there. When he came to England on his mission, he was arrested and imprisoned at Wisbech. He and some other men had escaped from there just a few months before he met with Sprott in Lincoln. When they were together at the Saracen's

Head in Lincoln, what had condemned them was the discovery of holy oils and some breviaries in their mail. The trial was a travesty, with no real evidence against them, and it has been remarked that there was nothing to show that they were priests at all, but Sir John Glanville ordered that they should be found guilty.

They met their horrifying deaths with fortitude, and the strangest events were to follow: the judge who had tried them died just two weeks after their deaths, and in July, John Glanville fell from his horse and died. He was a judge of the Common Pleas, and his instruction for the priests' deaths was one of his last actions. He may have had a reputation for fair dealing, but he was intransigent with the Catholics, and one wonders about these two deaths just after the brutal executions at Lincoln.

There were also the special courts: the ones set up by the crown for particular purposes. The most notorious one is arguably the Star Chamber, which was required when the law took on those with extreme power and status. The first reference to a 'Star Chamber' was at the end of the fourteenth century. It sat, in the years under discussion, at Westminster, with privy counsellors and influential judges taking part. Primarily, it was a court of appeal, and main encounters were with people of influence who had not been convicted, largely because of their status. It was about fair enforcement in both civil and criminal affairs; yet there was another dimension to its work: it was an opening for appeal for the plaintiffs of a lower social class to confront their offenders, and this was often something relating to moral as well as legal issues. Of course, such an institution could be very useful to a Tudor monarch who had enmity against anyone opposing his wishes.

At the point of the court's establishment, in the act of Pro Camera Stellata of 1487, there is an explanation of why it was to exist, and F.W. Brooks, in a study of the Yorkshire context of the court, wrote:

> The preamble to this act gives a vivid picture of the evils it set out to remedy. 'Whereas … by unlawful

> maintenances, giving of liveries, signs and tokens, and retainders by indentures … oats … and otherwise; embraceries of his subjects, untrue demanings of sheriffs in making of panels and other untrue returns, by taking money by juries, by great riots and assemblies, the policy and good order of this realm is almost subdued … to the increase of robberies, perjuries and unsurety of all men living and losses of their lands and goods …'
>
> In other words the court was to confront all kinds of abuses and corruption in the ranks of those entrusted with running and directing justice.

The Star Chamber was a significant and opulent event as well. As Susan Agee explains in her study of the court, 'After the business of the court was finished each Star Chamber day, an elaborate dinner was served at great expense to the state. The price of a meal rose from twenty pounds in November, 1590 to about eighty five pounds in June.' In modern values, £20 was equal to around £13,000. In 1500 £10 could buy one seven horses or twenty-six cows. Susan Agee also explains the role of the presiding judge:

> The presiding judge delivered the orders of the court and when necessary, required the attendance of the other justices. He sent cases to other courts and directed the cases which proceeded in the Star Chamber. Whenever the court's opinion was split, he delivered the tie-breaking vote as well as deciding the costs in all cases. The King addressed all letters to him whenever he wished to communicate with the high court.

The court was abolished just before the Civil War, and as Krista J. Kesselring has commented, we do not have the records of judgements: 'So, as we pore over the pleadings and proofs left in the court's own archive, we're very often left wondering what the judges decided. What narrative prevailed? Who was punished, and how?'

We do have some narratives, and in a now classic example of scholarship in Tudor studies we have the *Star Chamber Stories* by G.R. Elton (1958), and one story there, 'The Fool of Oxford', Elton tells the sad and muddled tale of a legal student and writer called John Parkins. The rare value of this account of an impassioned and probably unhinged man caught up in litigation is that we have some kind of answer to an important question about Tudor justice: what happened to people involved who were not rich and powerful but who nonetheless asked for help and guidance? Parkins was a lawyer at first, in the middle temple, and he wrote a book that was well received, *A Profitable Book Treating of the Laws of England* (1555 in English). Later, just after the Pilgrimage of Grace (see the next chapter) he was in Oxford, where he 'showed signs of a crochety and quarrelsome disposition and a mind disturbed into incoherence and even near-madness', as Elton expresses it.

The result was a sequence of letters sent to Cromwell, who was able to direct the Star Chamber, about the Abbot of Osney and other churchmen. His accusations about them began to point towards treason. Elton points out that 'the purport seems dreadfully clear: Parkins was hinting at knowledge dangerous to the abbot and was asking blackmail.' Here was a difficult situation for the Star Chamber, and before that might happen, it was dangerous for those who had power in Oxford.

What happened was that the Privy Council was first involved, and Parkins was on two occasions told to face questions, and then be shut up for hours to write down his actual opinions and evidence of any malpractice. When he had the chance to plead his cause, Parkins sealed his fate; as Elton explains, 'He alleged that the commissioners had their food and drink at the abbot's expense and were dining with them at Fleur's house. They were joined by others equally linked with the two monasteries …' In other words, Parkins was aggravating and coming across as unbalanced.

What was the fate of such a one enmeshed in the legal process in a high court? First, it was a spell in Oxford's Bocardo prison by the church of St Michael; he was also shut up in the old town hall, to write his complaints, and at one point he was physically bullied and then when in gaol he was pressed to admit that he himself was guilty of treason. Parkins claimed that he was 'exhibited at Carfax market, the crowd being directed to cast their eyes on a local troublemaker'. Elton comments that the commissioners had no love for the man but had to give him a full hearing. Two abbots in the area were being defended on a charge of treason, and the result was the ruin and shaming of the very mentally sick person who happened to be able to write on the law; he wrote many times to Cromwell, and at one time even said that a charge of buggery could be brought against the accused. The Buggery Act was in the news, as it were, being a statute of 1533. Buggery is defined as 'an unnatural sexual act against the will of God' and in the trials there was a closer definition – anal penetration and bestiality.

How did all this end? There was a meeting with Cromwell, who must have been tired of all the letters, and Parkins was simply told to 'live the mean life'. The conclusion was, then, that nothing was ever to be gained by accusations of the kind generated by a man who was accredited with no real social standing. The Star Chamber and the Privy Council were far happier dealing with large-scale fraudsters, robbers and abusers of extraordinary power.

The courts offered a complex mesh of litigation, and lawyers were always busy. Some research has shown staggering facts and figures about the crimes going on in this state on the fringe of Europe, where great empires were swelling with ambition, and with designs on the little island over the Channel. In his study of sex and sexuality in Britain through history, Richard Davenport-Hines gives this statistic: '… in Essex, with a population of about 40,000 adults, some 15,000 people were summoned to court for sex offences between 1558 and 1603'.

There has been no mention of another kind of court – the manor. This ancient institution, reaching back to the Normans, dealt with local matters at a court leet. This was an annual court held by a steward, with the manor being given a charter by the sovereign. It dealt with jury crimes of freemen within the area. But this was extended in manor courts, which could deal with breaches of peace, public nuisance, maintaining boundaries and fences and so on. Tying in with this comes the subject of custom, and in his magisterial accounts of law and custom, E.P. Thompson quotes a text from 1696 that sums up the nature of custom and how it relates to material becoming common law:

> For a custom taketh beginning and growth to perfection in this manner. When a reasonable Act once done is found to be good, and beneficial to the people, and agreeable to their nature and disposition, then do they use it and practise it again and again, and so by often iteration and multiplication of the Act, it becomes a custom; and being continued without interruption time out of mind, it obtaineth the force of a law.

With this line of thought comes the fascinating link between the attitude of 'we have always done this in this way' and something eventually relating to a stated legal principle. So we have the intriguing relationship between the law as established by statute and by judges in selected courts, and the common law, running like a stream of common sense from experience through centuries of life in Britain. When students of law read the Reports of Coke, they see the variance of readings in his weighing legal matter against actual events and actions of men and women.

What this survey of courts in the sixteenth century shows is that wrongdoers and accused, in all kinds of contexts, could soon be indicted; it was an easy matter to break the laws, because there were so many laws made, many covered by the string of statutes enacted by the Tudor monarchs. My survey concludes with a look at another kind of court which is classed as a minor equity court, which was a court defined separately from courts involving factors of common law. My example is the court of requests, created by Richard III in 1484, and the concept was a place where poorer people could be heard, and where costs were manageable. It became so oppositional to common law treatments that there was a certain frustration built into hearings, but this example is a special one, as it involved William Shakespeare.

The case happened in 1612, just outside my scope, but worth a glance into this time, just four years before Shakespeare's death. The case was Bellot v Mountjoy. The latter was Bellot's father-in-law, and had promised a settlement after Bellot's marriage to Mary Mountjoy in 1604. A dowry and another sum was still unpaid in 1612. Shakespeare lodged in Mountjoy's home in Cripplegate, and he had to make a deposition. He had known the married couple. In the end Bellot was awarded 20 nobles, but there is no record of this being paid.

What did such a case involve? There was always a basic bill of complaint (in fact, a petition); this was followed by a response from the plaintiff, then a reply to that, and a final rejoinder to the plaintiff. Shakespeare would have had interrogatories put to him. He was surely someone who was a kind of go-between, given his address. He would have spoken of both. Then he could respond to these questions before matters led to the final judgement. It is known that the poet spoke, alongside Joan Johnson and Daniel Nicholas.

The point to stress here, regarding the ordinary citizen and the law, is that several plain folk had to speak. They had to express themselves clearly and with a sense of the importance of what they were saying in the context. In my research into serious crime through the ages I still have the shock of finding out that not until 1898 could the accused, even when faced with murder, speak to the court. There was such fear in the ranks of defence lawyers that the accused would present negativity to the jury that silence was often the preferred option.

A summing up of this very broad and complex element in the law of this time has to stress that everyday working people were often involved in legal procedure, and their lives were no doubt lived at a certain level of high apprehension. Outcomes of criminal trials were acquittal, prison or death for serious crime. But there was, as with the case of Parkins, the other options – immediate punishment. This could be anything from the pillory to a public shaming, as with Parkins. What were absent were possibilities relating to the X factor of transgression: sheer bad fortune and human error, and that was sometimes a death sentence. After all, a survey of gallows in and around York *c.*1500 comes to fourteen in total, and there were courts keeping them busy. Power was local, embedded in long-established centres of power, and held in the tight grip of those who had wealth, land and influence.

Chapter 2

Order and Disorder

There is plenty of law at the end of a nightstick.

Grover Whalen

The fear and the faith fitted in very well with something much grander, more philosophical and much more important to rulers, lawmakers and those with any degree of higher powers. This was the idea of order, and not simple order in terms of things being in their proper place. Crime and sin were aspects of something much more fundamental for the medieval mind: the belief that everything in divine creation was in its place for a very sound reason. If everything in nature and everything man-made did as it was told and stayed put, doing what it should, then all would be well. Anything on the move, in transit, shifting to somewhere else was stirring up a divine harmony that extended to all God's creation, from the eagles flying at the limits of the sky to the worms delving deep in the soil. Even the concept of purgatory meant souls awaiting movement upwards and onwards to that heavenly place where they integrated into what was firmly in place; prayers were said for them – novenas and prayers in chantries where living loved ones of the dead spent cash to have their friends and relatives saved.

Transgression disturbed all this. When we recall one very important element in this scheme of things we see where crime and sin take on some stature in the ever-changing divine creation: this is the fact that the sovereign stood supreme as God's right hand being on this Earth, where fallen mankind worked to cope with original sin and with the weakness of mere mortals. In the Act of Supremacy discussed in the previous chapter it has these words, that the king would act, '… most to the pleasure of Almighty God, the increase of virtue in Christ's religion, and for the conservation of the peace, unity and tranquillity of this realm …'

The world was seen as a place in which great, all-embracing unities and elaborate cohesion of all parts had to be respected and maintained. Ideas of the whole universe, made by God, fitted in well with much earlier classical ideas about cosmology in which deities had their own patch in the great scheme of things. The author of the standard work on this world picture, E.M.W. Tillyard, explains this: 'The world picture which the Middle Ages inherited was that of an ordered universe, arranged in a fixed system of hierarchies but modified by man's sin and the hope of his redemption.' If the modern reader, with a secular turn of mind, finds it hard to accept the notions of the world order and redemption, he or she need only look to the land of India and the river Ganges today. Eric Newby, writing of that river, said this in 1983: 'To be cremated on its banks, having died there, and to have one's ashes cast on its waters, is the wish of every Hindu. Even to ejaculate "Ganga, Ganga" at a distance of 100 leagues from the river may atone for the sins committed during three previous lives.'

This because in the world of Henry VIII and of Shakespeare, the potency of belief in sins and of the afterlife was as real as the farmer's meadow or the knight's lance. The life to come was the genuine stuff of the human contact with, and immersion in, a full life of belief and spiritual conviction. So well organised was this ordered universe that in every order of life from the heavenly empyrean above in the distant skies, down to worm's domain of the earth, there was a hierarchy, a series of levels of existence. This matched well with criminality as well as with sin, for if a man was seen by his actions as on a par with a serpent or a lizard, a mouse or a louse, he was in a very low domain of the creation. If he was noble, heroic, admirable, he could be seen as a lion or an eagle.

This imagined great chain of being reflected the earthly doings and thinking of plain John or Mary in the streets or on the farms; the thought is expressed very clearly in one of the most widely known works of Tudor literature, *The Book of the Governor* by Thomas Elyot. In this he wrote:

> Take away order from all things, what should then remain? Certes nothing finally, except some man would imagine eftoons chaos. Also where there is any lack of order needs must be perpetual conflict. And in things subject to nature nothing of himself only may be nourished; but, when he hath destroyed that wherewith he doth participate by order of his creation, he himself of necessity must perish; whereof ensueth universal dissolution.

As far is law is concerned, some words of another Tudor thinker sum it up: '… of law there can be no less acknowledged than that her seat is the bosom of God, her voice the harmony of the world; all things in heaven and earth do her homage …' (Robert Hooker).

Another clear account of this necessity for order is in a work by William Tyndale: 'Let every man therefore wait on the office wherein Christ hath put him, and therein serve his brethren. If he be of low degree, let him patiently therein abide, till God promote him …' This was a version of what society could be and ought to be in a world in which political thinking could be applied well if only there was a general acceptance of 'knowing your place', as the old cliché has it.

What could possibly disturb this? Disorder, of course, was the answer. The works of theory saw crime and sin as being the threats, and naturally these took many forms. But open disorder in the towns was the most evident indicator of something wrong in the society at large. Some historians have made a determined attempt to answer questions about social disorder through the years of the medieval and renaissance period, and Samuel Cohn, in a study of popular protest, covered the years between 1196 and 1450, using chronicles and Patent Rolls as his sources. The chronicles accounted for over

200 specific incidents that were logged in the hundreds of towns in existence in the period. John Hatcher, in a review of the book, notes that the book covers, 'class struggles, riots against papal legates, colonial wars, riots of children, crown and town, tax revolts, poor against rich, burgesses against secular authority, church against city, conflict against bishops and universities, risings against Jews and foreigners, disturbances caused by heresy and Lollardy and many others …' In other words the years in question were tumultuous.

Instances of open disorder are not hard to find. Christopher Hibbert, the biographer and historian, gives a typical of social threat: 'In 1451 a gang of four hundred armed men rode into Walsingham during the sessions then being held there and secured the acquittal of all their friends.' He adds that: 'Bands like this became useful instruments in the forceful settlement of private disputes, in the prosecution of private vendettas and … in the frequent raids upon landed estates.' This was a mainly lawless society, and in the context of this event, we have to recall that the York and Lancastrian Wars of the Roses were taking place all around these small towns and villages like Walsingham. There may have been assize courts, judges and justices, but for everyday life, the limits of protection and security went as far as the night watch people, the justices and a constable.

There was a threat to public order and to the crown just a few years into the reign of Henry VII. The victor of Bosworth faced a rebellion in the north. Now known as the Yorkshire Rebellion, it took place in 1489. There were many causes of this unrest, including taxation to fund a war in France, demands made to maintain border protection, and much sense of palpable injustice. Robert Chambers led an assembly in Cleveland, and a gathering at Thirsk led to a stepping up of violence. Henry Percy, 4th Earl of Northumberland, was murdered. Percy was the Lord Lieutenant of Yorkshire and was killed at Cocklodge, probably because the crowd thought him to be against their situation.

A force of around 5,000 captured York, and the result was that Henry sent an army north. There was a fight at South Kilvington, and a considerable force went into the field. But the whole affair increased in scale and numbers, and later Sir John Egremont led a larger recruited force south towards Doncaster. Again, York had been taken, and the fear grew in the ranks of the court and the southern nobility. The uprising petered out with capitulation, and so began the usual treason indictments and executions.

After less than two months, the rebellion had been suppressed, and although some were hanged, others were pardoned. It was a case of a swift concession of defeat, with some insurgents running off to France. The rebellion opens up for scrutiny the issues behind the unrest, and historian Michael Weiss has summed up the wider issues: 'The rule of law and the loyalty to such a remote authority as the crown had no deep roots,' and Henry VII, 'sought to prune the excessive influence of the [Percy] family.'

In contrast, what becomes noticeable in the Henrician years after the king had applied a number of statutes and placed a high degree of fear within the actions of the law, is a determination to crush dissent, and for Henry VIII the fact is that he was to become the major force for disorder. This imagined world of the great chain of being was about to be shaken rattled and revised by the king himself, and the first of his revolutionary actions was the Dissolution of the Monasteries in 1536. If he thought that the Act of Supremacy, already discussed, would be a force for stability, he was very wrong. He needed funds. He was in debt, and his ambitions in terms of becoming a great European monarch to rival the likes of the French, Spanish and Holy Roman monarchs, needed funding. He looked around and he saw that there was immense wealth in the church. The evidence was clear to see in the religious houses and institutions. In order to find out what wealth there was in these places, Henry produced the *Valor Ecclesiasticus*, in English, the 'church valuation'. This was generally referred to as 'The King's Books' and it was compiled in 1535, dealing with England, Wales and some areas of Ireland. There was the question of taxes paid by clergy, and naturally the topic of owned material wealth.

The king had soon spent what money he had been left by his father, and the accustomed income from parliament was clearly nowhere near enough for him. This was only £200,000 over four years, and the future he envisaged for the regal life clearly would require far more than that. The modern word 'bling' appears to cover not only the gloss of wealth he desired on everything in life, but also describes the kind of lifestyle to which he aspired.

As usual, commissioners were employed to move around the land doing the inventories, and there was no room for dalliance and digression; they had a deadline of January 1535. It is stunning to learn that the men given these tasks of enquiry and monitoring of wealth were not paid, and just as impressive was the speed at which this data was assembled in books of records. One may imagine the benefits for the whole government of this information. Just as the *Domesday Book* had done by 1086, so the *Valor Ecclesiasticus* became a solid, reliable source of information. The movement towards crushing church power had taken off in earnest.

Not all the church establishments were grand and opulent. In Yorkshire, for instance, this is what was reported of Kirkham Priory in the *Valor Ecclesiasticus*:

John Kylwek, Prior. The site valued at 20s yearly. The monastery had a Cell at Carham, super Tweed	Total value, £3,000.15s. 5d Less Reprisals £31.9s 9d
Thomas, Earl of Rutland, Chief Steward received annually	5 0 0
Sir Marmaduke Constable, Knt. Steward	1 0 0
Alms distributed yearly on the day of the exaltations of S.Crux on the foundation of Guido Foster	0 14 0

Kirkham was surrendered to the crown, and in an instrument of surrender the list of people cast off includes a prior, a sub-prior, a deacon and twelve priests. In a letter from the Commissioners of December 1537 we have an insight into how such small-scale places responded: 'We have quietly taken the surrenders and dissolved … Kirkham … where we perceived no murmurs of grief in any behalf but we were thankfully received …' It is known that many of the priests were enjoying a pension in 1553, and that the prior had been given £50 per annum before his death (date unknown).

Even before all this happened, Henry had made abbots and priors take an oath that showed their acceptance of the Act of Supremacy; along with this came their support of the marriage of the king with Anne Boleyn, something that presented immense problems in terms of the allegiance to the Pope that the church leaders of course had.

There is no doubts that there was plenty of church wealth to acquire. In their notes on the Act for the Dissolution of the Greater Monasteries (1539), J.J. Bagley and P.P. Rowley explain there was a problem with assumptions of wealth:

> During the previous four centuries, first the monasteries and then, to a lesser extent, the friaries had grown rich. Rents, tithes, voluntary offerings, fines and fees provided most of their wealth, but the riches were so unevenly distributed that some communities were outstandingly prosperous and some comparatively poor. Less than half a dozen monks or friars in the smallest houses, and they had little influence on the life or economy of their area. Most laity and secular clergy had thought for years that these houses did not justify their existence …

The words used in the Act of Dissolution says everything about the attitudes behind it: 'The King our Sovereign Lord shall have, hold, possess, and enjoy to him, his heirs and successors forever, all and singular such late monasteries …' Nothing was to escape possession; places listed include '… in such like manner and form as the monasteries, priories, abbeys or other religious houses late by authority of parliament suppressed, have been ordered, surveyed and governed'. This was a recipe for disorder, and observers did not have to have military or political experience to see trouble coming. If there was a world order and a great chain of being which had to be undisturbed, then this would turn it all upside down. Questions were surely asked in every tavern and at every street corner. What about the Pope? When does Rome fit in? What will all the ordinary folk who work in these places do now?

Talk turned to plans; something had to be done. The king might be the Sovereign Lord but this was going too far with his power. Looking at this time, one may see the powerful contrast between Henry's rule and that of his father. Henry VII had needed to be always looking over his shoulder. There were claimants to his throne. He had to work hard to squeeze money out of those who had it. He had to grab the land of enemies and from those who had acquired land before and during the Wars of the Roses. He also had to find other ways to earn cash for his projects and plans. He also faced the limits of power imposed on him from the hurdles in his way in the form of the church and its jurisdictions. Some of the roots of Henry VIII's dissolving of church property may be seen in his father's struggles with church power. If an accused person could be tried in a church court rather than an assize, it was highly likely that he or she would be dealt with leniently.

Now came the rebellion. There was inevitable chaos and tumult in some areas of the land, and the leader who emerged was Robert Aske. The rebels, whose first assembly appears to have been in Louth, Lincolnshire, wore a badge of the five wounds of Christ. The king must have been worried, but he played the long game, and let matters progress, instead of sending an army to face the insurgents. Aske himself was Yorkshire based, and the rising spread to that county. Henry's plan of being deceitful and diversionary (even offering pardons) paid off, and the end was a heartless revenge and series of punishments on the leaders.

Aske was executed on the summit of the tower of York Castle; a letter to Thomas Cromwell giving instructions about the punishment and more correspondence followed until we have this account of traitors' deaths: 'The traitors have been executed, Lord Darcy at Tower Hill and Lord Hussey at Lincoln, Aske hanged upon the dungeon at York Castle, Sir Robert Constable hanged at Hull and the rest at Thyfbourne; so that all the cankered hearts are weeded away.'

T.P. Cooper, in his history of York Castle, adds this, '… it appears that it was the custom to hang traitors upon the summit of the keep at York. After the Battle of Boroughbridge fought March 16, 1322, the defeated leaders of the insurrection were brought to York and executed.' The revolt had been a crusade, as Simon Schama calls it, and he goes on to define the real significance: 'It was, in effect, the first act of the English wars of religion that mapped itself … as a Catholic north and west against a more reform-minded, or at least more heavily governed, southeast.'

Under Edward VI statutes were published abolishing all religious books apart from *The Book of Common Prayer.* Also to be removed were any images and icons of religious worship. These Protestant reforms were guaranteed to be the cause of widespread foment and protest. Before this there had been the 'Statute of Six Articles' of 1539, which became known as 'the whip with six strings'. This was Henry VIII deciding how he could put order and harmony into the religious lives of his people; it was an act that would cause tremors in the ranks of anyone believing in the freedom of conscience, the right to worship as an individual wanted, and it attempted to shape and form the subjects of the realm into one uniform, same-minded body of citizens. It was about 'unity' and aligns with notions of the chain of being and with the need for social cohesion, but of course it would create quite the opposite. The source of the king's fears are put clearly: 'the manifold perils, dangers and inconveniences which have heretofore in many places and regions grown, sprung, and arisen of the diversities of minds and opinions, especially in matters of Christian religion'.

This formula for suppression and the erasure of individual minds would suit a despot. Principally, all subjects were to believe in the blessed sacrament and that there 'remaineth no substance of bread and wine nor any other substance but the substance of Christ' and 'the very flesh' and 'the very blood' are 'as they were both together'. Also listed were celibacy of priests, chastity vows and private masses.

The impetus behind all this is patently concerned with trying to remove the various kinds of disturbing issues highlighted by Lollardy and other disturbances of the desired equilibrium of the brave new world of *do as you are told* at the base of royal power. The Act was repealed under Edward VI in 1547.

The uprisings came thick and fast through the decade after the church was subsumed into the powerhouse of the crown; there was a rebellion in Cornwall and also Jack Kett's open challenge to the state in East Anglia. Mark Stoyle has argued, in new work, that the Cornish trouble was actually very nearly a successful coup that could have easily put an army in London, bent on destruction. Foreign mercenaries came just in time for the royal forces to take victory. The event became known as the Western Rising, and began in Sampford Courtenay in June 1549, then spreading to Cornwall. Stoyle wrote: '… there was a rapid mobilisation of and advance by large numbers of Cornishmen. This would have made the combined forces of the rebellion far more dynamic, assertive and threatening than has previously been recognised.'

In the end, Lord Russell, who received the help from the mercenaries just in time to sway victory his way, managed to beat the rebels at Fenny Bridges. Even at that late stage in the progress of the revolt, hundreds of rebel reinforcements were arriving from Cornwall. As Stoyle sums it up, 'It was a desperately close thing.'

A look at a sequence of entries in the State Papers for 1549 tells a very enlightening story. The following summaries tell their own tale of fear and reprisal:

July 23: … order prescribed by Lord Grey for the executing of rebels in Oxford and other counties; some of the priests to be hanged on their own steeples.

Oct 1: Sir Thomas Smith to Cecil: deplores the evil state of the realm; suggests the appointment of one or two responsible gentlemen in each shire to enforce the King's proclamations. The watchmen are the great promoters of rebellion. Lord Grey's men are worth 10,000 proclamations.

Oct.1: The King to Sir Henry Seymour: warrant to raise men to Hampton Court. Bring them to the Court without delay to suppress conspiracy.

Signed by the King's stamp

This all has a tone of panic about it, and it makes one see again the desperate measure of making a proclamation. That word begins to seem increasingly like a fearful expression of a last command as the enemy are at the door.

In contrast, Kett's rebellion, beginning in July 1549, was a matter of land, fences and enclosure; when fences were destroyed by the workers, Robert Kett, an employer of men, not a rebel, saw the case of justice and wrong at the heart of the problem, and became a leader rather than one of the mob. A sizable army of dissidents set up their base at Mousehold Heath close to Norwich. The core of the unrest was a simple fact of the pressure of social change. Landowners keeping sheep wanted more pasture, and they fenced the land, so that opposition against them grew. Even the church was against the process.

Norwich, the second largest town in the land at the time, with around 12,000 people, was besieged, and even more of a triumph was the rebels' defeat of an army sent by Edward VI to confront them in late August. The whole business was not to last, however, as another national force led by the Earl of Warwick crushed Kett's force at Dussindale. The formidable fortress of Norwich Castle was be the place of Kett's execution at the end of the year. All this sprang from the basic need for more wool production in the economy, and was in a manner that was to be increasingly familiar in Britain in the coming two centuries or more: the constant pressure to expand land for animals at the cost of both common land and traditional agriculture. The issue was to be evident in the works of the Augustan social commentary verse as much as in the writings of the satirists and politically engaged writers of the Romantic period.

In Kett's surge of revolt, the fences in place at Attleborough, as common land was enclosed, was the kernel of unease. There were so many illegalities across the land after the regime of Henry VIII and his statutes and proclamations that drama and performance had been one casualty of freedom of artistic expression. That expression could so easily be seen as subversive, and a monarch conscious of any kind of offence was responsive to the power of public theatre. Consequently, a performance of a drama at Wymondham about St Thomas Becket was asking for trouble. The events after this celebration at a feast show exactly the kind of complex local repercussions of the Henrician Reformation, because a local landowner called Sir John Flowerdew (who sounds like a character from *A Midsummer Night's Dream*), had been an objectionable figure after his part in erasing Wymondham Abbey, and now here he was, partaking in fencing as well. His only move was to offer cash to be left alone, so the first wave of rebellion met with a victory.

The leader, Robert Kett, was in a long-established Norfolk family. After understanding the discontent, he helped to ruin his own fencing and led the mob to their campaign of destruction. Today, Kett's leadership is a significant local heritage, and the county council played their part in preserving the location of Kett's Oak, where the rebels met, though the oak tree that was there has long gone. The first movement and consolidation of the rebel force was at first only met by county dignitaries, who apparently thought that a verbal appeal to reason and practicalities would have some effect. But there was an escalation.

The former St Leonard's Priory became Kett's base, and more people began to swell the ranks of Kett's force. At gatherings and discussions, they came up with a list of their reasons for unrest and thought that sending this to someone of important stature would achieve some kind of notice and appropriate response. Edward VI was still a young adult at the time, and the protector was Somerset. There were all kinds of displeasure and ill feeling in the masses of protesters, and apart from the enclosures, there was the subject of serfdom – something close to slavery – and the problem of vagabonds (a subject in a later chapter here). There had been another statute in this very year of public discontent, touching on the problems of wandering labour and free movement of workers. A writer not long after this revolt wrote of the vagabond problem: '… and he so called when he goeth first abroad; either he hath served in the wars, or else he hath been a serving man, and weary of well doing, shaking off all pain, does choose him this idle life, and wretchedly wanders about the most shires of this realm …'

At first, with this horde of threatening and violent people encamped and gathering support, a pardon was offered for a capitulation, just as Henry VIII had done; but the insurgents were asking for all kinds of reforms, so many that the world of the Tudor realm would be upturned. There had to be a military solution, and it came. What really lit the fire of extreme response was a determined and extreme attack on Norwich itself, and after that there was an attempt by Lord Sheffield to confront the rebels. After an initial possible agreement, there was a tough face-to-face fight, and Sheffield was cut down. Now there was serious trouble coming Kett's way. His nemesis was to be the Earl of Warwick.

Again, as in Cornwall, there were European mercenaries in the ranks of Warwick's army of around 14,000 fighters. The rebels fell back when they saw the superior numbers in the force against them, simply burning property and trying to detract from a direct scrap. Warwick forced a retreat and Norwich was regained. The end came for Kett and his men at Dussindale; their backs against the wall, Kett and his men had to accept defeat. Though Kett was taken at first to the Tower, his end was to be in Norwich. Estimates reckon that 3,500 of Kett's followers lost their lives in the rebellion.

Designs of man's life on Earth and the structures of the divinely created world of Earth and cosmos are all very well on paper and in the seminar, and politically it would have been a dream of the Tudor lawmakers that every breathing being in the Lord's creation would do as the law told them. However, in reality the world follows its own course, and the individual's hierarchy of needs follows such matters as hunger, sex, death and the demands of daily work and duty. Statutes multiplied and sovereigns came and went, but the urgency of feeding one's family and of satisfying lusts as well as social aspirations would create transgressions great and small. As had been the case since people first lived in communities, there would be self-help and there would be social caring, but things were tough. Life expectancy, the fragility of the body and vulnerability to both local and national events, from plagues to the sweating sickness, all happened without dependable defence and protection. London was a long way from the Scottish and Welsh borders, and Ireland was no more than a marginal part of the crown's concern.

Riot and disorder unsettled everything and constantly challenged the defenders of social security and the rule of law when there was very little to use in facing that challenge. There was no policing. The citizen needed to carry arms and know how to use them; disorders came from within the citizens as well as from armed men and dangerous criminals. In this atmosphere one would expect murder and serious assault to be common as turnips.

Was this the case? How easy was it to avoid the noose or the axe in Tudor life? My next enquiries follow these questions.

Chapter 3

Bloody Murder

For man's grim justice goes its way
And will not swerve aside:
It slays the weak, it slays the strong,
It has a deadly strike.
Oscar Wilde

As so often when one looks at the criminal offences in a specific period of time, murder takes centre stage. If we use the word homicide instead, that concept steps up the enquiries we make into trying to find out how violence plays a part in social relations at a given time. Murder is commercial. Stories of atrocities done from person to person open up so many rare insights into society and its components, that what we today call true crime, and the crime reporting in the media, have always been persistent factors in news, gossip and the interplay of knowledge and opinions. These form the social gel, playing a part in holding together moral views and sustaining social norms. An account of crime and law in any context therefore has to place murder, the act of intentionally taking a person's life, centre stage.

Readers and students know something of the nature of violent crime in the sixteenth century through literature and popular culture. It was in the Tudor years that the printed book in Britain emerged, with the success of William Caxton (1420–92), who made the first printing press in the country at Westminster, and his authors printed included Chaucer, Sir Thomas Malory and John Lydgate. This made it possible for cheap narratives of crime to be printed, and of course, criminal tales were popular in the early forms of stories and ballad produced. Shakespeare and other popular Elizabethan dramatists made crime prominent elements in their writings, and in some plays, murder featured as a subject for exploration, notably in *Macbeth, Julius Caesar* and *Hamlet.* The motivations explained and explored in these works show that a profound interest in murder has always been at the core of society's interest and concern. With this in mind, the status of and fascination with wilful killing was often in focus in the stories running through everyday life, in work and in recreation, from the mystery plays and touring dramas. In an intriguing letter to *The Times* in 2025, Philip Womack wrote that 'After Christopher Marlowe's *Tamburlaine* successfully toured Shropshire in the seventeenth century, several little boys were christened after the play's hero, including Tamburlaine Davies, who became High Bailiff of Ludlow.'

Sometimes historians take on a seemingly impossible task, and one of these is the attempt to know and understand the nature of violent crime. One of the most enterprising and enlightening of these is Lawrence Stone, who over forty years ago tried to come to some conclusion about the extent of interpersonal violence from the fourteenth century to the 1980s. If we attempt to understand that topic in the sixteenth century, his guidance about linking such data to the wider societal issues is a sagacious angle on things: 'If most early modern homicides were outside the family, this pattern is repeated in litigation, which also shows a very high level of personal animosity between non-family members.' He backs this up with a comment on the situation in Tudor times: that, in the words of one reviewer, we are 'sighing with relief that one did not have to live in these gossip-ridden mean-spirited endlessly litigious and generally rather nasty villages'.

What emerges from Stone's reflections on what evidence there is about such violence, leads to thoughts on the concept of anomie. He wrote: 'What all this suggests is that between 1560 and 1620 there was an abrupt increase a wide variety of indicators of social anomie and of a breakdown in consensual community methods of dealing with conflict.' Émile Durkheim's theories of anomie relate to multiple factors which he saw as he wrote at the end of the nineteenth century, including mechanisation, the estrangement of individuals in community groups, warfare and revolution, and perhaps most of all, an increase in isolation of people as societies emigrated from formerly well-settled societies. One only has to look at the example of Ireland in the decades from the 1840s (the years of the potato famine) to the end of the century. In Tudor terms, if we look for sources of anomie, one aspect is clearly evident – the migration of labour from the fields and parishes.

Shakespeare, as is usual, has some words for this. He notes, in *The Taming of the Shrew*, one seemingly universal reason when Petruchio is asked why he is away from home. He says such 'winds that blow further from at home/where small experience grows' but this ascends beyond the reasons notable in economic terms, closer to the Grand Tour than to poverty. The economic wellbeing of the country was in the mind of Henry VII after Bosworth, when he was making decisions about new legislation, and he was aware of what S.T. Bindoff, has described: 'The leading measures … sprang directly from that complex of changes, agrarian, industrial and commercial … which itself reflected the quickening tempo of the nation's economic life.' Bindoff mentions several statutes enacted between 1489 and 1497 which all worked in some way as protectionist, and one of these – the Acts of 1489–90 against enclosure – showing the fears behind what was to develop later.

Anomie comes from a sense of being disconnected, afloat and belonging to no social validation of the individual selfhood. There is a strong sense of the confrontation between injustice and social disintegration in one of Shakespeare's most philosophical plays, *As You Like It*, which was completed in 1600. Shakespeare sets up a court society run by Duke Frederick, and an exiled, rural-based group headed by his brother, Duke Senior. The society depicted is one in which the hard, dictatorial and despotic court has driven away a slice of the realm, and an erasure of traditional values that have held society together are being ruined by autocracy. The aged servant, Adam, who is cast away and rescued by the central figure of Oliver, describes the regime that has cast him off:

> Know you not, master, to some kind of men their graces serve them but as enemies? No more do yours. Your virtues, gentle master, are sanctified and holy traitors to you. O, what a world is this, when what is comely envenoms him that bears it!

Duke Senior, in contrast to the people in the court back at his former home, lives with like-minded friends, and in his first words in the play, he says something that defines a theme that Shakespeare wanted his Tudor theatre-goers to consider:

> Now, my co-mates and brother in exile, hath not old custom made this life more sweet than that of painted pomp? Are not these woods more free from peril than the envious court?

As Alan Brissenden, the editor of a recent edition of the play, comments, 'The disharmony of life outside Arden [where the Duke Senior is exiled] … is reflected in the dislocations of time …' In other words, Shakespeare imagines an anti-society in which attitudes are very much like the hippy beliefs of the 1960s in the USA. Shakespeare saw many things wrong with the England of Elizabeth, his queen, and dislocations explain one aspect of these ills.

The 'dislocations' appeared continually through our history. Two hundred years later, Jonathan Bate, writing about the poet John Clare, made this point about enclosure, and how the 1801 Act had made general enclosure universal:

> For many villagers, enclosure was experienced as an engine of social rather than economic alienation. Use of the commons was technically a right restricted to those who occupied certain properties but psychologically the unenclosed spaces were perceived as belonging to everyone. Enclosure was therefore symbolic of the destruction of an ancient birthright based on co-operation and common rights …

Anomie is everywhere in the literature of the Tudors, and it is no accident that explorations of the individual self-emerge and grow in the literature and prose of the time, when we see, through modern eyes, centuries after major wars and revolutions, that anomie is created through disintegration and the uprooted nature of much life on Earth under various autocracies.

The violent society Lawrence Stone and others have described related perfectly to the estrangements and oppositions in the literary heroes of the time. That does not mean that a murderous society will follow, but a look at some particular murder cases of the years between Henry VIII and early Stuart times will reveal some elements in this disintegration, and the world of 'endlessly litigious and rather nasty villages'.

An account of murder and the society around the crime has to look at the legal and communal factors, and for the sixteenth century this includes such subjects as the means of escaping the noose, who will conduct the trial, what part violent behaviour played in the offence, and what part was played by basic forensics. Not only were there several legal influences on these matters, but there was the intricate matter of the social status of the perpetrators, assumptions about gender, constraints on those wielding power, and other factors relating to the processes of justice and investigation. Even what we call forensics was naturally at work, and Blessin Adams, in her account of the murder of Richard Hunne in 1514, which I explain later in the chapter, shows in detail what an investigation into the crime scene achieved.

The normal process of investigation has one outstanding feature that the modern reader will notice: it involved personnel, and this was in a time with no professional police. Questions about who actually was involved in matters of investigation, questioning and arrest will occur constantly in tales of bloody murder or extreme violence at this time. For instance, people in power, such as Wolsey or Thomas Cromwell, who had to act at the highest level in a process of crime investigation, had their 'myrmidons', as one historian called them. These were referred to throughout historical reporting as *poursuivants*, and this was a term used for the sovereign's messenger. In fact, these shadowy figures figure in press crime reporting through the centuries. In the period of revolutionary fervour and fear of treason under the Georgians they are mentioned as undertaking arrests of radicals. They were notably involved in the arrest of turbulent politicians and satirists through the years, and the beginnings of the messengers extend back to the time of Richard III. V. Wheeler-Holohan, a former messenger himself, explains:

> The earliest trace of the appointment of a King's Messenger simply as a King's Messenger and nothing else, that I have been able to trace is dated in 1485, and is in an Original Writ of Privy Seal, confirming the appointment of John Norman to be one of His Majesty's Messengers and ordering the arrears of his salary of 4 and a half pence per day to be paid to him …

In the will of Anthony Conwaye, one of Elizabeth's messengers, dated 1568, we know of one messenger, and there had to be a body of men in these ranks in order for them to be effective in pursuing serious crime, and sure enough, Wheeler-Holohan notes that there is a nominal roll with forty names in the records of the Lord Chamberlain.

This was surely an invisible police force, acting as messengers for the crown, and in between as officers of the law.

The first cases under scrutiny are those of Christopher St Lawrence and the murder of Richard Hunne. The first is a case of extreme cruelty and the second one of murder.

Christopher St Lawrence, the 8th Baron Howth (*c.*1509–89) is a highly contentious figure with a mix of political acumen and family brutality in his less than envious CV. He became a lawyer, entered at Lincoln's Inn, and as he became active in politics he assumed a position of opposition to what was Elizabeth I's attitudes and laws concerning Ireland. He became known as the 'Blind Earl' but there appears to be some uncertainty about whether or not he had lost all his sight. What helped him immensely to become a person of power was his entry into the Privy Council and his growing importance in Ireland, which at that time was composed of the wild Ireland of the earls, and the supposed extension of English power and settlement in the area around Dublin known as 'The Pale'.

The Pale was established by law in 1488, and a map of that area shows that on the coast it extended from a little north of Clogherhead, down to Bray, known today as a seaside venue south of Dublin. Inland it stretched to Athboy and Clane, and to the north, as far as Kells. This is important in the story of Baron Howth's life and career because he rose to be a negotiator with the clans, was supported by the queen, and knighted. He began his Irish identity as a representative of the crown with some problems, and for his acts of opposition he was imprisoned for some months before being redeemed and placed back with some power still, but he had questioned the tax on The Pale, known as the 'cess', and lost his image as faultless ally to the queen and parliament.

A key question regarding his status and his actions is the nature of The Pale. The historian Steven Ellis has come to be an influential writer on the subject, and his arguments about the area being much more successful than previously thought were expressed well by Ruth Canning in a review of Ellis's book on the English Pale. She wrote: 'Central to this study are three assertions: (1) the Pale was not a failing entity; (2) it was undergoing expansion, not retraction; and (3) the Pale actually satisfied the impossible Tudor goal of anglicising its indigenous Irish residents.' This is useful information in understanding how and why the Baron was in place and had to be trusted. He was a successful figure in Irish life, but the aristocrat at home was a different character entirely. He had to operate in a context of military fractiousness too. Steven Ellis wrote: 'Old English landowners were alienated by the burden of maintaining an enlarged English army and the abrasive conduct of army captains ...'

A note from the law courts helps us to understand the nature of Ireland at the time. It was seen as a punishment at court to send a criminal off for military service in Ireland, and in Kent, for instance, several men were sentenced to compulsory service. In 1602 Thomas Amys, a horse stealer, was in a situation in which the grand jury did not find a true bill. He was sent to serve in Ireland. Richard Punchyn was a bigamist who had forged a death certificate so he could marry a third woman. He, too, was sent to serve in Ireland.

Switching to the family and household of this outwardly admirable man of his time, we find the Mr Hyde in the Baron. What broke the bad news to the public as well as to lawyers was developments in the trial of Nicholas Tyrell, one of his servants, for perjury. It emerged that the Baron was alleged to have been extremely cruel to his wife, Elizabeth Plunket. Sir William Gerard, the Irish Lord Chancellor, pressed the case and a trial was held in the Irish Star Chamber, known as the Court of Castle Chamber. The trial demonstrates the situation about where alleged accused persons could be tried for specific offences. The Castle Chamber was supposed to be primarily for cases of disorder but this does not really apply here. On the other hand, domestic cruelty, which is what was alleged, was normally something for the church courts to deal with.

The law at the time regarding husband's violence towards their wives was influenced by the 'duty of obedience' and the thinking was that a man could exercise 'moderate correction' in his treatment of her. The difference between a beating and the breaking of a limb must have played a part in judgements regarding that phrase. But the Baron thought his beatings were normal for a husband's behaviour. The old rhyme 'A woman, a spaniel, a walnut-tree, the more you beat them, the better they be' seems to some up common attitudes. Lord Wilson, in his law lecture of 2012, explains the thinking behind this element in social history:

> … the law then, according to some legal historians, introduced a rule whereby a husband was prohibited from beating his wife with a stick or rod thicker than his thumb. So here, if this theory is correct, we find the rule of thumb. The husband's right of moderate correction of the wife was abolished only in 1891.

That last sentence is shocking through modern eyes, and we could add to that the fact that only as recently as 1991 was there a ruling that a husband forcing sex on his wife was guilty of rape.

But for whatever reason, the Baron was tried there, at Dublin Castle. The charges were grievously cruel and brutal: the scenario was one of repeated physical assaults on his wife; she had ran off, away from him at times, and the most horrendous attack was when he gave her such a beating that she was unable to leave her bed for some time. The narrative of his cruelty is even more extreme when it comes to his daughter, who was only in her teens: he whipped and beat her on her back, as was done in military punishments, according to one assessment in a Regency account of the case. This daughter, Jane, died of the wounds. He was a killer as well as a merciless, degenerate torturer of those he supposed to love. He was not your everyday criminal, who would have been destined for the end of a rope, so when he was found guilty, the punishment was a fine and a few months behind bars. He lost his family and had to pay alimony.

The Baron and his wife had had fourteen children, but only a few of them lived lives of which we know anything of any substance; their father married a second time, this time to Cecily Cusack, who outlived him as he died just after the marriage. It might surprise people to find out that the Baron went back into public life for a while, still leading those who wished to oppose the relentless pressures of a government wanting to increase the taxes on The Pale.

It is helpful in understanding this case to reflect on the fact that Queen Elizabeth herself explained why a court that was supposed to be concerned with public order and riot became a place for such things as family issues and charges. She wrote: '… we have thought it meet to appoint that a particular court for the hearing and determination of those detestable enormities, faults and offences shall be holden within the castle of Dublin.' The court had been created in 1571, as the general opinion in London was that the Irish courts then existing were not up to the task of anything demanding the kind of rigour England expected.

It certainly would have experienced some shivers of revulsion when the Baron's deeds were recalled.

Turning to the sad fate of Richard Hunne in 1515, we have to refer back to the discussion of Lollards in my introduction, as it was his Lollard beliefs that were largely responsible for his murder. The root of his fight with the church was staggeringly trivial. After his baby son died shortly after his birth, Hunne had to give the church the child's christening gown as payment of a mortuary fee. However, he refused to hand over the gown. On the surface, for a man to be imprisoned and eventually killed for such an offence seems to be the very worst kind of punishment in a world in which life was cheap and religious convictions very expensive. That is, it cost – in so many ways – when a person stood against the tide of an increasingly intransigent and heartless law machine.

As Blessin Adams points out in her account of the case, Hunne 'may have been an upstanding citizen, but he trod a dangerous line as he made no secret of his disdain for religious authority …' When the rector, who had been confronted by Hunne from the start, decided to take his complaint to a high court – the Court of Audience at Lambeth Palace, many would have been astounded at such a small-scale matter of a baby's mortuary fee being a cause of such escalation. The fact that it did transfer to such a higher legal echelon is, in fact, fully understandable when one looks at the constant concerns about vengeful uses of courts right across the board of legal provision. Ruth Goodman, in her survey of people behaving badly at this time, devotes three solid chapters of discussion and case studies all relating in various ways to insults, offence and disobedience. She sums up: 'Laura Gowing found 2,224 defamation cases that were brought to court in and around London between 1572 and 1640. In a city with around 100,000 inhabitants, this represents a steady trickle of around 30–40 a year.' This points to a society in which status, social hierarchy and reputation were rated very highly, and that insults and offences were easy to commit. Hunne's rector had been challenged on a matter of church behaviour and custom. The result was that Hunne was shackled and taken to the Lollard's Tower in St Paul's.

What followed was a sequence of events that led within two days to his body hanging in his cell. What followed was some forensic questions of a very impressive nature, to do with the silk binding on his neck, evident blood smears and body position. The coroner, Thomas Barnwell, was the most accomplished investigator of the crime scene from a juryman group, and they found a murder, not a suicide. The culprits were found: three men who had been cruel and determined to the extreme; Hunne had been tortured and fasted, and one of the aggressors had been the principal instrument of the actual murder – a certain ruffian, assisted by the others, who were more reticent. But it comes as no surprise to learn that the case against them was dropped.

In early Henrician years, the church was acting with extremist fervour and a disregard of suspects' rights. Hunne was a Lollard, and that was beyond acceptance. He was the enemy within, as far as the church was concerned. To have punished the killers was tantamount to rewarding a dangerous dissident.

These two cases are instances of the possible extremes of injustice and avoidance of just punishment possible in the Tudor courts. The first was an aristocrat who had the power of a cruel manorial lord over his own flesh and blood, and the second was a comparable brutality and heinous violence against a parishioner of a church that was supposed to behave with Christian mercy and understanding, rather that apply vindictive violence against a good man.

Murder cases were only one aspect of a culture of male violence; virtually everyone carried arms, and street fights were a regular occurrence. Violent deaths were consequently commonly not defined as murder but as manslaughter, and there were various circumstances in which proving a deliberate intention to kill was hard to accomplish. One of the outstanding locations in society for this culture was around the theatres. Any search of the lives of playwrights will very likely bring up tales of deaths in brawls or arguments, spells in prison, and factional squabbles. A case in point is in the lives of two writers linked to the theatre outfit called The Admiral's Men: Ben Jonson and Thomas Dekker. The former's works are still quite well known, and the latter figures on the margins for anyone studying Elizabethan drama.

Jonson was a turbulent character: born in 1572 and dying in 1637, he is recorded as being a soldier and a bricklayer, but his talent as a writer for the stage extended to both tragedy and comedy. His work had also caused him problems: his play *The Isle of Dogs* not only provoked the authorities to visit the theatre and do some damage; it also led to his being imprisoned in the Marshalsea. One of his theatre friends, Gabrial Spenser, seems to have been a hothead, always in trouble; he had fought with a man called Feake, and Jonson had stabbed his right eye and then Feake died. Luckily for Spenser, associates gave character references, and after all, the business was a disagreement in the world of artistic types, through the eyes of those who knew the hostile jealousies and oppositions in that subculture.

But in 1598 Jonson met Spenser, and yet again there was a confrontation. This was in Shoreditch, and the fight became so heated that the man with the more lethal weapon, Spenser, should have had an advantage, but was drunk. Jonson's rapier ran Spenser through the body and Jonson was a killer. He was arrested and found himself in the infamous Newgate gaol. He became yet another literary man whose neck was saved by the benefit of clergy. He was a scholar, and not only did he know Latin, but he knew plenty of biblical content, and key phrases of the 'neck verse' were easy for him say. The words appeal for mercy, and he got it. As Catherine Arnold, the historian says in a blog post, after noting that Jonson was recorded as a bricklayer, 'Jonson, no doubt, would have been hurteth greatly to be referred to as a bricklayer, the trade which he despised.'

This tale has plenty of drama. A more typical character from the theatre world would have been Thomas Dekker, who could be described as a jobbing writer, having been employed to work on play scripts with others, and his actual original work is hard to define. But he is recalled for his play *The Shoemaker's Holiday* of 1599. His later works, in the early Jacobean days, were failures. Poor Dekker, like so many of his peers and social circle, was very familiar with the insides of debtors' prison, and he spent seven years in the King's Bench prison. Seven years behind bars at that time would have killed most people, but he somehow survived, and did more writing until his death in 1632.

The most notorious murder case from the theatrical world is that of Chistopher Marlowe, (1564–93) author of successful dramas such as *Dr. Faustus* and *The Jew of Malta*. In one poetry anthology, he is referred to as 'one of the great revolutionary poets of the Elizabethan age' and the same editor states what most reference works do: 'The Privy

Council issued a warrant for his arrest, but, almost at the moment they did so, he was killed in a tavern brawl at Deptford.' We now know, mainly thanks to the research of Charles Nicholl, that the circumstances of his death were more complex than being in a brawl.

The death and its surrounding scenes and characters involved has become the subject of television documentary as well as of serious historical research, and we now know that his death occurred when with supposed friends, and at the hands of people he would have trusted. This has led to speculations about Marlowe's involvement with spy networks and with powerful men of the Elizabethan age. Charles Nicholl, in *The Reckoning*, asserts the essential truth about one of the most pertinent facts behind the actual killing, and this involves Sir Robert Cecil, spymaster. However, he adds a note of caution: 'The involvement of Sir Robert Cecil in the immediate background of the Marlowe investigation has not been known before. We should not jump to conclusions and assume some sinister involvement.' But what now seems certain, after some modern forensic minds have been applied to Marlowe's death, is that it appears to be likely that his 'friends' were involved, and he died with a blade to the brain.

The facts of the scenario of the death are well established. On 30 May 1593 a group of men met at a house (not a tavern) in Deptford Strand. They argued about the bill, according to the words spoken in defence at the inquest. From this one argument, Marlowe was alleged to have had a knife in his hand, and Ingram Frizer, the man charged with committing the murder, needed help to disarm him. The defence statement records that in the scuffle, the blade went through Marlowe's eyes to the brain. As Nicholl concludes, 'The blood and the scream are not the coroner's concern. He simply records that Marlowe died "instantly".'

Another writer of the time, Thomas Kyd, is recorded as saying that Marlowe had 'rashness in attempting sudden injuries to men' and though Nicholl doubts that this implies physical violence, he admits that he thinks Marlowe 'a scoffer, rather than a brawler'. Yet, however we try to assemble facts and inferences to that Deptford death, the result is that Marlowe enters the historical records as a tempestuous character, always likely to be involved in trouble. Nicholl challenges the reliability of the inquest as a reliable source, but he admits that the narrative there has been accepted through the years as 'there is no provable alternative'.

The Elizabethan stage people and the culture of violence form the backdrop of all this, and this provides one of the clearest examples of what tends to happen in a society where citizens carry arms as a regular habit. If one needs an instance of the general consequences of this, one of the plainest ones is in *Romeo and Juliet*, where the members of the Montagues and Capulets have a confrontation that happens by stages of insult and coded aggressive speech. Regarding the fight between Jonson and Spenser, much of the unhappy result of this is explained in the words of Giacomo di Grassi's work of 1595, *The Art of Defence,* in which he wrote:

> The sword and buckler fight was long while allowed in England … but now being layd downe. The sword but with serving men is not much regarded, and the rapier fight generally allowed, as a weapon most perilous, therefore most feared, and thereupon private quarrels and common frays soonest shunned.

There is one more angle of interest here, and that is in the matter of 'maiming'. This term is related to the word 'mayhem' and refers to a specific act of violence which is defined in law as 'The violently depriving another of the use of a member proper for his defence in fight'. In such a violent age as the sixteenth century, and equally previously in the York and Lancaster wars, what the law calls 'violent affray' entailed this avoidance of a probable murder charge, because the thinking was that a wound such as the cutting of muscles to stop movement was a neat way to disable and so weaken, opening up differing explanations in court. This became an important element in the law of offences against the person in what became known as the Coventry Act of 1671. Peter Burke, writing in the 1890s, explains the origins of this, referring to a vicious attack on Sir John Coventry in the reign of Charles II:

> Horror at this atrocious outrage … induced parliament to bring in at once, and to pass within a few days, a bill enacting that 'Unlawfully cutting out or disabling the tongue, of malice aforethought, or by lying in wait, putting out an eye, slitting the nose or lip, or cutting off or disabling any limb or member … with intent to maim or disfigure, shall be felony without benefit of clergy. That is, subject to capital punishment …'

There are several ways in which this Act opens up some understanding of the nature of brawls such as the street fight in *Romeo and Juliet*. The first reflection is that obviously we may conclude that for centuries the disablement of maiming would have provided doubt in judge and jury regarding the aggressor's motive. In the context of a brawl, it is an easy matter to argue in court that blows, hacks and slices of a blade were effected in a rough and desperate way, with the intention being a blurred notion. Another factor is that a maiming would win the fight without further threat to the aggressor. The word 'affray' could cover so much disparate activity.

The maiming could result in death in a hotheaded quarrel, of course. Long before the defence of provocation and the complexities of self-defence there was the concept of 'chance medley', which created a term and a line of thought for a death resulting from a sudden contretemps; this was what we know now as voluntary manslaughter, and it was a standard defence in cases of a death in a heated and violent encounter. The words of guidance were '… the casual killing of a man, not altogether without the killer's fault, though without an evil intent; homicide by misadventure'. It was all a question of where the moral culpability lay.

Bernard J. Brown wrote about this in a discussion of the two Latin terms used in law: *se defendendo* and *se infortunium*: defence or bad luck. Brown adds that these were treated on an equal footing 'until the eighteenth century, treated for purposes of punishment … whilst the former gained recognition as a justifiable act, the latter remained until the early nineteenth century merely an excusable one, on conviction for which no corporal penalty was imposed.'

Shannon McSheffrey discusses a chance medley in Hereford in 1511 in which Henry Baskirville died in a knife fight at the hands of Roger Lloide. She points out that the word chance was sometimes spelt as *chaude* (hot in French) and that Lloide had run into a churchyard, knowing that possibly sanctuary was maybe his only chance of avoiding immediate arrest. Lloide in fact ran away into outlawry, which meant he was in deep trouble, but McSheffrey thinks that he was pardoned in 1514, and the decision was a chance medley.

Chance medley was yet another way of handling those homicides that were done in a tangle of emotions and actions over quarrels of honour, reputation, heated accusation, and so on. Bernard Brown adds a footnote to his above article that provides a convincing account of proceedings: 'It appears that special verdicts for justifiable and excusable homicide had fallen into disuse when Foster was writing (*c*. 1762) and that judges were accepting general verdicts of acquittal in cases of killing *se infortunium* and *se defendendo*.'

Murder and varieties of homicide were thus acts that could enter the cloudy, unsure realm of accidental events in a culture of general violence. Murder, in comparison with a cluster of other offences related to general fights and enmity, has always been the highlight of judicial definitions and explanations, and Thomas de Quincey understood, in his classic essay on murder, why avoidance of the offence, the covering up the specific intended crime, has been a manageable thing: 'If once a man indulges himself in murder, very soon he comes to think little of robbing; and from robbing he comes next to drinking and Sabbath-breaking and from that to incivility and procrastination.' The strenuous efforts of those who are capable of planning to take a life and then to really do so are the stuff of crime fiction as much as of true crime stories, but it is often forgotten that the tales of making a death interpreted as something other than murder have long been found in the pages of legal history and in millions of court records.

There is also the factor of bias through the history of murder trials. Reading such records, the historian surely concludes that there is plenty of evidence for the argument that prejudice survives all evidence in many instances. Certain trends and tendencies reoccur in criminal history, such as the commonly accepted comments in regional cases that such and such a jury will not convict. This was a factor in my own research into a Welsh case in the 1860s which I have recorded in *The Girl Who Lived on Air*. But added to this is the power of the judge, as in cases heard at the assizes for instance, where a 'right' verdict was expected. In the Tudor years, who could possibly have acquitted such accused as the leading rioters and voices of dissent in the social upheavals of the 1530s?

The fact that Richard Hunne's killers in the Lollard's Tower were allowed to go free comes across to modern readers as offensively, morally wrong. The context of the particular power base of the church in 1515 makes the fact of this bias hard to accept, but it is sometimes hard to disagree with Rousseau in *The Social Contract* when we read court cases from centuries back: 'Laws are always useful to those who possess, and vexatious to those have nothing.'

Chapter 4

Everyday Offences, the Bench and Bridewells

There are only about twenty murders a year in London, and not all are serious – some are just husbands killing their wives.

Commander Hatherill of Scotland Yard, in 1954

Shifting from national and major cases in crime to the business of the officers of the law in a more workaday context, the focus moves to the offences before the magistrates. What were the offences most commonly before these upright citizens, who had to cope with everything from public nuisance to the common thefts and larcenies to be found everywhere? The Tudor years were a dizzyingly busy time for them.

A look at a typical Quarter Sessions record will show just how much work and responsibility sat before the bench. This is an early Stuart example, but the material is very much the same as it was through the Early Modern years. On this agenda in 1620 were: hues and cries, churchwardens' accounts, constables' accounts, conveying of cripples, relief of the poor, bastard children, local land assessment and individual criminal cases. The session was held at Barnsley and the bench included Sir Francis Wortley, two other knights and two gentlemen. Presented for judgement were people mostly in the dock for small thefts, but other offences open up some important aspects of local justice, such as:

> Richard Stead and Roger Willans for … refusing to aid and assist Edward Smith and John Blagburne, constables … in the prosecution of one John Thornton for felony (confesses: fine, 6s 8d)
>
> William Newbold, scissorsmith, John Thompson, carpenter, and Robert Dixon, collier … for assaulting there … George Saunderson, and maltreating and detaining him in prison, until he paid a fine of 5s to the said William.
>
> John Roberts of Barnbrough, yeoman, for not attending with a musket, for the service of the King, the musters held at Rotherham.

Through twenty-first century eyes, these three cases represent notable insights into the nature of the criminal law at this time: the imprisonment and abuse of a debtor, when compared with the 'false imprisonment' offence of today, linked with physical assault, is extremely serious. In the case above, they were found not guilty. The refusal to aid a constable tells us a great deal about the tough and demanding work undertaken by constables, and the muster roll offence speaks volumes about the general fear of protection and communal security at the time.

Other duties before the Barnsley bench were the tricky topics of land value assessments, care of the infirm and elderly and other matters that today would be the concern of the social services. One heartening aspect of this is in the case of two aged people threatened with eviction by landlords. The bench ordered their lives in the properties to continue, but added 'if the owners of their said houses will consent'. If not, they became a problem for the overseers of the poor.

Mixed in with all these daily small affairs there were the serious offences, and transferrals to York Castle. Through modern eyes, the thought of murderers being handled alongside minor assaults and thefts is quite staggering. The Tudor refinements and advances in processes of trial and pleading were, as is so often the case in crime history, largely either pragmatic or something relating to the latest statute, and the benches were adjusting accordingly to the generation of law.

What were some of the broader issues, then, attached to the everyday criminal offences and how they were seen and tried? For the Tudor bench, it was a case of pros and cons – the familiar topics of bastardy, small thefts and minor punishments such as branding and whipping, by the side of the murders, serious highway robberies and the new offences that kept on being defined, such as the 1533 Buggery Act or the Witchcraft legislation.

To understand this question, and some of the answers, one could shine the light on Kent in the 1590s through to the early years of James I. In Kent for the years 1595 to 1609 there are depositions and gaol delivery rolls that give quite full information about offences. The real diurnal substance of Tudor crime emerges from this evidence, and once again the modern reader has to reflect on a society with no police force, a focus on local community cohesion and the fact that some leaders would appear who could pursue and sometimes catch offenders.

A deposition states an accusation or an opinion regarding an offence, and gaol delivery relates to the action taken by the travelling judges at assizes, so we see in these documents only glimpses of a particular crime. But the depositions may be very informative. At the time of my own research into crime in East Yorkshire in the 1790s, I found a solid cache of depositions regarding alleged cruelty to a child in an area close to Beverley. The magistrate would have had plenty of information to use when he enquired into the people involved.

The patterns of these crimes in Kent have three significant features: opportunistic theft from homes; burglary and assault in the home; and organised gang activity, notably for rural crime such as deer poaching and sheep stealing. Clothes were commonly stolen, along with animals and any small objects that could be sold. One case records feathers being cut from a pillow and taken to be sold. What crops up as attempts to avoid punishment (often branding) are benefit of clergy and benefit of the womb.

What stands out is a total reliance on the help from neighbours when subject to an assault or to burglary; a community had to be held together by bonds of social allegiance, instinct of self-defence and a need to survive as a group, each supporting another, and being in readiness if there is any intrusion. The records here for Elizabeth's last decade on the throne show a society in which little children cut purses among groups of adults at church; where strangers may enter a home and assault people at will, and where anything that can be picked up and carried away will be lost if there is the slightest opportunity for the smallest level of larceny. Of course, dwellers in places such as Ashford were close to the direct travel routes to Europe, and wandering soldiers were often open to rob wherever they could.

Even without the police, perpetrators were often taken, as this record, a statement by a labourer, shows:

> He saith that he saw the said Ellin in the howse standing behind the bed, and another woman with her and that they had broken a cupboard and a chest and that they had out of the cupboard 7s 4d in money and that they had heaped together his wyfe's clothes ready to be carried away, that they brake the window … and when they saw that they were founde, as he watched for them at the window, they opened the back dore and went out where shortlie after they were taken.

The nearest official in existence was the borsholder, who was the head of a tithing (a family unit). This made him an underconstable, so he was one of the few men in a community who had a responsibility to protect and do duties that would link him to the work of magistrates. The tithing was a group of ten men, in a unity reaching back to Saxon times, who stood security for each other. That is, they were a framework for reaction to any problem. Clearly, they did; a borsholder came in to help with the case of some stolen sheep, and the thief was found in his home, hiding the evidence.

Evidence for the vulnerability of the average householder is not hard to find. In 1601 in Ashford, before noon, a man entered the home of Tabytha Adams, and he was later joined by another man. Tabytha managed to go into a back room and shut the door, but she was threatened with assault, and in desperation escaped through a window. The men '… did draw out her mother's drink into pots and pales and carried forth … and they all together did drink and continued lingering about the house until a sister by chance came thither and rebuking them, threatened to complain to the next justice …' They left and headed to an alehouse.

Tabytha must have been terrified, but the reports suggest that this was not an uncommon event. On one occasion a number of women were arraigned and appeared before the bench after stealing from a private house. Here we see the dubious benefit of clergy at work. After the hearing, the Quarter Sessions gaol delivery reads: '… all guilty, and read as clerks and burnt on their left hands.' There were eleven women in the group, standing in court. They had been saved from a serious punishment by the benefit of clergy, as they 'read as clerks'.

The nature of the 'neck verse' has been touched on before, but here we see its universal use as an escape from a noose or a long spell in gaol. The problem of the accused being able to read the lines from Psalm 51 'Oh God have mercy upon me, according to thine heartfelt mercifulness' may have actually meant something back in medieval days when Henry II had confronted Thomas Becket with the issue of secular and church courts being a major problem in the justice system, but by Tudor times it was merely a way out of extreme punishment. In 1512 Henry VII had made offences defined as 'unclergyable' and these included 'murders and felonies upon malice prepensed' – hence my previous discussion in the last chapter on homicide. By 1530 another statute moved to stop a second appeal for the benefit of clergy, and that was for chance medley. There could be no second benefit for murder, treason or any felony. Then, by the time of the women in Kent being allowed the benefit and then branded, many more offences were on this list, including rape, poisoning and witchcraft. If the women had entered the house in the night hours, and committed burglary, they could not have been given the benefit. Matters relating to the benefit were becoming very much against leniency by the early years of the seventeenth century.

Increases in the scope and workload of the justices were happening frequently through statutes in the years of the Tudors, and as Bertram Osborne points out:

> It was a bad time for many of the rapscallions of the period: As the arm of the law extended, more and more of them found themselves, for the first time, within its reach: offenders in hunting by night, (1486), deceitful makers of feather beds (1496), users of crossbows (1503), mummers (1512), killers of weanling calves (1537), witches (1554), makers of foul and fantastical prophecies (1573).

This was all work for the magistracy, and their work extended into regulation in many areas of life as well as in criminal affairs. Licensing took up a lot of their time, and also supervision of the highways and public nuisance; renegade soldiers and deserters, travelling beggars, and universal of all problems in front of them was arguably that of wandering labourers, the begging poor and all varieties of people on the move. It was a problem that extended back through the centuries. J.J. Jusserand, writing a century ago, explained the issue very neatly, referring to a hundred years before the Tudor period: 'Statutes multiplied in vain; the king was obliged to recognise in his ordinance of 1383 that the "feitors [idlers] and vagrants overran the country" more abundantly than they were formerly accustomed.' He also asked all local law administrators to have the stocks ready for the wanderers.

The local gaols might not seem much of a threat, but Jusserand goes on to cite one case that is a truly horrendous depiction of what the arms of justice could inflict:

> Assizes held at Ludingford. The jury present that William le Sauvage took two men, aliens, and one woman, and imprisoned them at Thorlestan, and detained then in prison until one of them died in prison, and the other lost one foot, and the woman lost either foot by putrefaction. Afterwards he took them to the court of the lord the king at Ludingford to try them by the same court. And when the court saw them, it was loth to try them, because they were not attached for any robbery or misdeed for which they could suffer judgement. And so they were permitted to depart …

One needs to be reminded here that the ever-increasing work of the justices to work on the plethora of repressive statutes under the Tudors is because we are dealing with a series of monarchical regimes that sought to suppress rather than alleviate the restlessness that macroeconomic circumstances caused. Karl Marx put such a situation in these words in his *German Ideology* of 1846: 'But the more these conscious illusions of the ruling classes are shown to be false and the less they satisfy common sense, the more dogmatically they are asserted and the more deceitful, moralising and spiritual becomes the language of established society.'

From the establishment of the English Reformation with Henry VIII at the head of everything relating to civil and legal power, crimes were always going to be many and frequent, and the work of the hard-pressed local bench shows this; there is no better way to understand this than to look at what was happening with measures for imprisonment.

Fundamentally, until the middle years of the Tudors, prison was simply for immediate local problems or for keeping offenders somewhere secure until the assize court came to town. This meant that no one particularly cared about such topics as safe custody, sanitary provision or proper care. The thinking was, in a world in which the everyday offenders were no more than an annoyance, either speedy physical punishment such as branding or whipping or the use of lock-ups to keep the criminals out of sight would be the only needed provision, other than for serious offenders, who would wait for the gaol delivery. These attitudes and actions caused all kinds of humanitarian problems, mainly through the prevalence of death through typhus or other diseases, starvation, deprivation or deadly neglect. There were always stocks standing by. For the crown prisoners waiting for trial, there was also a sheriff's dungeon available, and that was another makeshift 'county gaol' before any proper organisation emerged.

A typical example may be seen in the penal provision in Gloucestershire. Since the thirteenth century, the town had watchmen for night patrols, and holding offenders in these circumstances entailed using lock-ups; a summary issued by the Gloucestershire museums and archives service notes that their lock-ups were 'small stone or brick built building with one or two small cells'; there were such places in Bisley, Cirencester and Westerleigh. There were also gaols for debtors, and treatment was supposed to be better for these people, but in practice the same dangers were under the roofs of the places of detention.

Then, after an Act of 1576 in the reign of Elizabeth I, came the houses of correction, or bridewells. This was a penal revolution;

Quarter Sessions, with their magistrates and local landowners, were to build these in order to fulfil the state intentions of setting the idle beggars and wanderers to physical work. The origin of the bridewell term was in the use of the royal palace of Bridewell in London. John Stow, in his Survey of London of 1598, explained how this became a house of correction:

> But now you shall hear how this house became a house of correction. In the year 1553, the 7th of King Edward VI … Sir George Baron, being mayor of this city, was sent for to the court at Whitehall, and there at that time the king gave unto him for the commonalty and citizens, to be a workhouse for the poor and idle persons of the city, his house of Bridewell, and seven hundred marks land, late of the possessions of the house of Savoy, and all the bedding and furniture of the said hospital of the Savoy, towards the maintenance of the said workhouse of Bridewell, and the hospital of St. Thomas in Southwark.

In Gloucestershire, there is an instance of the sense of using space available, and integrating new with old. The old castle facilities were beyond use, and the place was described as 'a ruinous place saving some few rooms for the keeping of common prisoners, the gatehouse and public workhouse …' Two more bridewells were established, at Winchcombe and at Lawford's Gate. The idea of the house of correction being a workhouse was essential; they were to be places of industry and there was no room for idlers. As time went on, the supervision of the magistrates became more and more important, and there was always an eye to potential profit. The revolution in all this was in the concept of having the drifters and grafters assembled in one place, supervised and fed, disciplined and given time to hear sermons. It was to be a place where one would work, eat, sleep and pray. It also has to be recalled that staffing was not a case of professionalism. In my study of Northallerton, which began life as a house of correction before becoming part of the national penal provision in Victorian times, the whole of prison development may be seen, from its being a local gaol for the sheriff in the thirteenth century all the way to being a twentieth-century military gaol, borstal and general male prison.

Students of the houses of correction have dug deeper into their nature and rationale. One of the most thorough and wide-ranging accounts of this is in the work of Austin Van der Slice in his essay back in the 1930s, when he looked at some relevant context for the new gaols. He pointed out the European dimension, with a startling opening to his essay: 'In 1589 the bench of aldermen of Amsterdam objected to pronouncing the usual death sentence for theft on a sixteen year old boy. They urged the burgomaster to find a better way to deal with juvenile offenders.' The answer to was the founding of a house of correction. Slice describes the organisation, and this reads very much like the words on the walls of the York female penitentiary from later times – that it was a 'house of care':

> a board of regents consisting of four burghers met regularly each week to supervise the government of the institution. There were to be likewise two townswomen who were responsible for the diet and household economy. There was a resident warden whose wife assisted by two servants performed the housework. There were two spinning-masters, a rasping-master, a school teacher and a medical man …

In this way the usual structure of running the bridewells began to be in place. England followed suit, very much in step with the Dutch advances. There were still punishments, and the death penalty was still present in the Dutch model, but the notion of care took precedence in plans and practices of administration. In Northallerton, for instance, two centuries and a half after the first bridewell, the house had a cook, a teacher, a parson, a visiting doctor, workshop leaders, gate staff and staff caring for the young. After all, women gave birth inside these walls, inmates died and medical care was always needed.

There is no underestimation of the trouble caused by the proliferation of people on the loose, out of their parish and turning up somewhere as 'aliens' as they are often recorded in the legal documents. Austin Van der Slice gives a vivid picture of the threat and the punishment, under Henry VIII in his 1530–31 Act:

> Under the act impotent beggars were to be licensed by the justices to beg within certain limits. All vagabonds and beggars without such licence were to be stripped to the waist and whipped until bloody, or set in the stocks for three days and three nights on a diet of bread and water. They were then to be sent to the place of their birth or last three years residence and set to work … For the second offence this punishment was repeated and in addition they were to stand in the stocks and have one ear cut off. For the third offence … they were to lose the other ear …

Shakespeare created his criminal characters in many of his plays, and in *The Winter's Tale* he gives expressions of their methods of work and income: 'To have an open ear, a quick eye, and a nimble hand, is necessary for a cut-purse; a good nose is requisite also, to smell out work for the other senses. I see this is a time that the unjust man doth thrive … Every lane's end, every shop, church, session, hanging, yields a careful man work.'

Popular works appeared, educating the general public in the subcultures of crime. In William Harrison's *Description of England* of 1587, he lists names given to these classes of offenders, such as 'rufflers, uprightmen, hookers, rogues, priggers, palliards and fraters.' Clearly, books such as this give the modern reader enlightening insights into the social world around the ordinary person in Tudor times. For instance, open-air performances of such things as popular dramas and miracle or mystery plays had always been the haunt of thieves, but 'cozening' or committing fraud, was everywhere practised, it appears, and again, popular works were in print explaining the threats to the good people of towns and villages where the wandering thieves would gather.

There might have been brutal physical punishments for theft and for simply being a wandering, rootless peasant, but there was an even darker side to this than ears being cut off. Christopher Hibbert puts the situation succinctly: 'But up to the middle of the sixteenth century many men were mutilated and some were hanged for little worse than idleness.' He adds that the numbers hanged cannot be ascertained, referring to the massive figure of 72,000 quoted by John Stow, but he does mention Bishop Rowland Lee, Lord President of the Council in the Welsh Marches hanging 'thieves in hundreds, right and left'.

Petty criminals could also be subject to public humiliation and physical punishment, and Hibbert mentions yet another such repulsive punishment given to vagrants: 'An Act of 1530 provided that vagrants of both sexes were to be tied to the end of a cart, naked, and beaten with whips … till the body shall be bloody by reason of such whipping.' He adds that the infamous Judge Jeffreys once ordered: 'I charge you to pay particular attention to this lady. Scourge her soundly … scourge her till her blood runs down. It is Christmas – a cold time for madam to strip. See that you warm her shoulders thoroughly.'

This was Tudor Britain: a place in which justice was primarily defined as punishment and law-breaking seen as one step away from chaos and anarchy if it was not strongly suppressed. To read biographies of both ordinary and indeed prominent people of that century is to see how close they often were to prison. What strikes us now is how fragile was the local community, how open to assault, to ruin, to destruction; in addition, how sensitive and assailable was an individual's reputation and public image within their trade, profession or calling. The importance of clothes, public appearance, reputation, all made the individual person subject to anxiety and the family unit sharply reactive to anything that might tarnish their image. Once again, Shakespeare has the right words for this, spoken by Rodrigo:

> Reputation, reputation, I ha' lost my reputation. I ha' lost the immortal part, Sir, of myself, and what remains is bestial ....

The church courts were often concerned with 'reputation' and the idea of an 'immortal part' is not stretching things too far.

By the time of the last years of Elizabeth, there is something more substantial to deal with the social crises caused by these factors for unsettlement in the community. The watchmen, tithings and underconstables were simply not enough to cope with the consequences of large-scale economic change, and the root problem was poverty and the 'idle poor'. What happened was the Poor Law. Although the Acts themselves were effected in 1597 and 1601, for over half a century, at local level, there had been plenty of work done in this area of thinking about help for the poor. After all, there had been plague, hunger, extreme deprivation and even the threat of war, to say nothing of the series of bloody suppressions of dissent often ending in death at the stake or the axe.

This new step towards solving at least some part of the problem of the wandering types and desperate outcasts was the Poor Law. When one considers the desperate situation of another side of crime at this time, the dangers of the highways, it is plain to see that something more general was needed. As Bertram Osborne notes, in his history of the magistracy, 'It was these deserted highways that were the scenes of the outrages, murders, robberies and other violence, that were so common an experience of travellers who ventured from one part of the country to another.' The thinking must have been that offering some kind of stability to at least some of the lost and threateningly desperate people who robbed through necessity would have been some kind of alleviation.

As S.T. Bindoff put it neatly, 'The first article of the Tudor creed that a united England was an invincible England …' had been shown in the defeat of the Armada and the end of that conflict with Spain. There had also been the endurance required to cope with the plague. At the time of the first Poor Law (1597) there was plague. It was always a threat. In 1572 a third of the population of Norwich fell victim to it, and in 1563 a quarter of the population of London had perished. Another serious outbreak came in 1603, and Peter Ackroyd, in his biography of Shakespeare, points out that the Bard himself was in an area hit hard by the pestilence; Shakespeare was living in Silver Street, and, 'Silver Street itself was not immune to plague. In the course of the epidemic a royal musician, Henry Sandon, died together with his daughter. A painter, William Linley, succumbed with his wife.'

The Poor Law Acts of 1597 and 1601 were radical in many ways, and there is no doubt that crime and the burdens of work put on the local justices were major influences in the thinking and planning involved. The Act of four years earlier had established overseers, and the roots of the system modern readers might know from reading Dickens are there; the impetus of most interest for reflections on crime and law comes from the need to instigate something other than punishment. The stocks and branding, and even hanging, were clearly not the habits of law enforcement to maintain and support. Previously there had been both taxation in some parts, and things such as church charity, in the church collection box and so on.

Yet it was not all about criminals and threatening footloose people; there were those who were defined as 'impotent poor' and this was largely a matter of care and attending to sickness. The almshouses and workhouses, as in the bridewells, were stage one of what the later centuries would know as 'the workhouse' as something only one step away from a gaol.

There were two types of people in the bridewell. Those who were able bodied had to work; hence the bridewell idea was the provision there. But their place was not actually to be in a prison. That was left the category of pauper labelled 'the idle poor' and they were defined and treated as prisoners in the bridewell. Work was the key to all the notions of reform. Even the children of the paupers were to be apprenticed to a trade.

There was cost involved, and so what was called outdoor relief was a simple option, as it meant feeding and clothing work for labours in the open air; unlike the later workhouses, there was a recognition of the importance of keeping nuclear families together. This was part of the effort of thought and consideration applied in this Act, as the basis for operation was by the parish, and many parishes were around the church, so local overseers were close to their charges, as was the case with beadles later on in the story of the rootless poor. The important central concept was that there should be a state of settlement – that a person or family being absorbed and placed in the parish would be part of a settlement, and this involved costs.

With this in mind, it is important to see that whatever was set up, there had to be a stress on things produced, earnings and basic resources. A perfect situation was a workhouse with the facilities of a small factory, and with supporting provision such as medical and caring facilities and staff; along with this would come the people who ran the show, attending to materials, training, religious observance and discipline. In fact, one may see in this the beginnings of what was to be the creation of more modern and efficient houses of correction in the late Georgian period, and even in the 1877 reforming zeal in the minds of the men behind the new prisons which would be the basis of the prisons built within the modern panopticon structure, in which there was constant observation of inmates. The thought was always to rely on silence, religious instruction and hard physical work – all elements of Tudor thinking too.

The highways might still be dangerous places, and the wandering poor were not immediately wiped out, but on the eve of the accession of James, the first of the Stuarts, there was at least a parochial system that aimed at absorbing the poor and offering more than the whip and the brand to them. Many must have thought, when they contemplated the old legislation that handled the problem with violence and fear, that neglect in the stables never made a better horse on the course. In practical and economic terms, governments were also coming to see that a superfluity of manual labour running loose and causing anarchy was a waste of manpower. Even 300 years later, on the eve of the Anglo-Boer War, the leaders of the state saw that the recruits for the forces of the Empire were not all fit and healthy, but were products of all the problems of the Industrial Revolution. In Tudor terms, these men and women were products of hunger, neglect and social disintegration.

The new laws for the poor were one small step towards changing this parlous situation.

Chapter 5

Getting Out of Gaol Free?

Twenty pounds were offered, under a Royal Proclamation, for the arrest of a priest, and one hundred pounds for the arrest of a Jesuit.

Joseph H. Hirst

Mary Tudor came to the throne in 1553, and until her death in 1558 there was an about-turn in matters of religion which was to bring heresy, blasphemy and treason to the fore. Mary married Philip II of Spain. Andrew Barrow, in his history of the Church of England, gives an example of what had to change – swiftly and noticeably – under the new Catholic regime:

> On October 1, Mary was crowned queen in Westminster Abbey. The ceremony was performed by Bishop Gardiner assisted by ten other bishops, all in mitres. The Bishop of Chichester, John Story, who had quickly shed his wife on the Queen's accession, preached a sermon. At the banquet afterwards in Westminster Hall, the seventy-nine-year-old Bishop of Durham, Cuthbert Tunstall, who had recently been restored to Durham House in The Strand, sat on the Queen's left.

History has a way of stopping one in one's daily tasks and routines, and Broad Street in Oxford demonstrates this perfectly. A memorial there reminds walkers and shoppers that three men, Cranmer, Latimer and Ridley, who had been kept in the Tower of London were now tried and found to be heretics. Archbishop Cranmer summed up his crimes, as Andrew Barrow sums up: 'Standing between armed guards and leaning on a staff, the white-bearded Archbishop declared his disbelief in the doctrine of the Real Presence and the Mass being a sacrifice for the sins of the living and the dead …' Latimer and Ridley were burnt 'on the north side of the two in the ditch over against Baliol' in 1555, and Cranmer in the same place in March the next year.

Cranmer had been one of the prominent men who played a part in the church free of Rome, being close to Henry VIII. He was charged with both heresy and treason under Mary, and before any torture was applied, recanted his earlier beliefs, but when the end was going to be at the stake, he recanted what he had abjured, seeing that his terror had ruled his actions. The prospect before him was indeed horrendous, in anyone's definition of a violent death. History gives a vivid and dramatic account of his fiery end – holding his right hand into the flame for a fast burn; this was the hand that had signed recantations.

The reign of terror under Mary was about to swing into effect, but before that, there had been a series of crises. The young king Edward VI had died, and the group of aristocrats backing the claim to the throne of Lady Jane Grey had her placed in the Tower, protected and ready to rule, with them backing her and indeed ruling through her. It was not to last. When what was seen as a coup to power was moving, Mary set up in Framlingham in Norfolk, and one of the leading rebels, Norfolk, was outplayed in his bid to oust her. The fight was not extensive nor successful and Mary, with an army of around 30,000 people, took London; Jane and Guildford Dudley, who would have been her consort, were taken, imprisoned and then tried. They were executed, and the reign of Mary began, but as usual problems and insecurities came with it. No sooner was she in power than the first challenge came along: the rebellion of Sir Thomas Wyatt.

Mary married Philip II of Spain. Her husband was not to have any regal powers, and was to be consort; the Protestant lords did not want this, and revolts were planned, but the only real threat was from Sir Thomas Wyatt, who marched on the capital from Kent with a few thousand followers. There was a much more disturbing challenge at one point when Norfolk with a force of men joined the rebels, but Mary did what Henry VIII had done twenty years before: she wrote a proclamation and offered pardons for dispersal. In the first month of 1554 Wyatt and followers were defined as traitors. A familiar pattern of suppression was in action. Even Elizabeth, her sister, and future queen was thought to be involved in the Wyatt revolt. She was kept under arrest in Oxfordshire for a year.

Mary, who has gone down in popular history as 'Bloody Mary', and her reign of terror needs some reflection in terms of the nature of crime and transgression in the period between the 1534 Act of Supremacy and the end of Mary's reign in 1558. This reflection requires the kind of empathic insight that those decades need. If we imagine the lives and thoughts of those in Tudor society who could and did talk, discuss and reflect on the changing regimes in those years, we have to consider the consequences of the string of statutes and the dictats on behaviour which flowed down to parish level and to the business of the magistrates. Those citizens who could read, think and converse on the orders of those new laws must have thought that the embedded notions of an ordered universe with God and the angels at the heights, and the Devil and his crawling creatures in the basest earth were disintegrating. After all, part of the basis of rule and security at all levels was the sovereign and his or duty to care for the subjects of the realm.

Where was the care? Where was the security? Older folk would simply know that regimes changed, monarchs died, and what was central to everything they thought and did – Christianity and worship in particular – changed seemingly like the Tower guard, every day. What could be relied on regarding their inner spiritual sense? Looking at this time through twenty-first century eyes and sensibility, one needs to imagine a microcosm within the world of the Reformation that was on shifting sands when it came to how one should worship and what could be official belief and what could not. Every corner of parish life was controlled and directed. Those with advanced years or with long memories could recall the times when there were certainties regarding church behaviour and what words were acceptable for use in that holy place. It would also have appeared to these citizens that even people of the higher ranks of the social hierarchy had been suffering at the hands of those in local power.

There was also the matter of the old beliefs and the Pope in Rome. When Henry VIII became head of the church in England and broke moral strictures that had been there since before the days of the Normans, it must have seemed like Britain was 'going it alone' in respect of how the craft of worship and man's relation to the Almighty was being steered. Related to this was the topic of violent deaths and bloody punishments. Kathleen Chater, in her really helpful book of questions and answers related to the Reformation, *The Reformation in 100 Facts*, puts the heart of this suffering most brutally, from the Catholic angle:

> The church would investigate whether individuals be persuaded to abjure their previous faith and comply with Catholic requirements. If they could not be convinced or were later found to have lapsed they were handed over to the secular authorities. Most were then burned alive; it was intended as a warning to others …

There had to be a high level of pragmatism in society, given the reliance on the parson and the magistrate to hold things together as the changes came and the new laws were formulated. The offences most noticed and punished on a small scale were dealt with by church courts and the Quarter Sessions, but compromise and understanding were applied. No doubt many ordinary working people held deep and sincere beliefs about the sacrament, heaven and hell, ghosts and devils, and what Jesus meant to them. If roots embedded in the medieval Catholicism of their grandparents still had a place in beliefs and thinking, then attitudes to crime would have some foundation, no doubt in the basic legal attitudes nestling safely under the word 'custom'.

When we shift focus to crimes in the higher reaches of society in an age of social unrest and rebellion such as the reigns of Mary and Elizabeth (covering the years 1555–1603), what is found is a level of brutality that makes modern sensibilities and moral compasses shudder. Under Mary, the law we recall most powerfully was all about heresy. Heresy was a crime with a long reach and a wide definition. When the infamous Spanish Inquisition set to work in Europe it was basically against any so-called evidence of unorthodox belief or behaviour; coming from a word meaning 'choice', the definition helps us to understand its application. That is, the accused chose the wrong and unacceptable option. The usual treatment of those unfortunates who chose wrongly in matters of faith and worship was generally a public shaming, so that there could be recantation and expression of changed thinking. Between Henry VIII and Mary there were various definitions of the word and the act of heresy, but there was always the idea of ordered, dictated actions and behaviour. Obedience to whoever was in authority was at the heart of regulation and suppression.

One explanation was given by G.K. Chesterton of the heresies Mary and her henchmen confronted: the variety referred to by Chesterton when he wrote, 'The heretic … is not a man who loves truth too much … The heretic is a man who loves his truth more than truth itself. He prefers the half-truth he has found to the whole truth …' The Marian regime was sure that it had 'the whole truth' of religious meaning and practice.

The mindset behind the generation of concepts of heresy may be seen in the wording of a foundation text of the term and its application. This is in the Edict of Thessalonica, and the dictat issued by Theodosius and others slips neatly into the minds of authority in 1555: 'We order the followers of this law to embrace the name of Catholic Christians; but as for the others, since, in our judgement they are foolish madmen, we decree that they shall be branded with the ignominious name of heretics …' The tool of heresy in the application of this heinous measure of torture and insistence on uniformity was reinstated under Mary in 1554 after being wiped out under Edward VI. The authoritarian foundation required under the Marian regime was one that, for modern readers, stretches across genres as well as years into the literature of dystopian repression of the worst kind – the variety of imposition that seeks to erase independent thought and to create a population of conformists who were told that there was no need to think beyond what was prescribed.

Heresy in this way became a blanket term, but in regard to the victims involved, it becomes entirely understandable why it is that the words 'reign of terror' are used repeatedly, and the catalogue of victims describes the very limits of brutality, such as the death of John Hooper, Bishop of Gloucester, as Andrew Barrow explains it: '… who had been held in disgusting conditions in the Fleet prison for the last seventeen months was burnt over a slow fire in his diocese. It took three quarters of an hour for him to die and at one moment he cried out "For God's love, good people, let me have more fire!"'

We only need recall the death of John Dudley, Duke of Northumberland, to understand the destiny of those who committed treason. The occasion was one of high drama; on his way to the block, this happened, as recalled by the chronicler of the Tower, Sir George Younghusband:

> At the Bulwark gate the Lieutenant of the Tower handed over the prisoner to the sheriffs of London for execution. It was here that out of the crowd came a woman who flourished in the Duke's face the blood of the Duke of Somerset and cursed the author of his death … The Duke

> first putting off his gown of swan coloured damask walked to the east end of the scaffold …

We have to turn to more universal aspects of Tudor imprisonment in order to understand the other side of such themes – the treatment of prisoners. At the core of this is the concept of *habeas corpus* – the writ processing the trial or inquisition regarding a person's reasons for imprisonment and related subjects of interest when one realises that this writ linked to the more humanitarian elements in maintaining a penal system. Paul D. Halliday has made a detailed study of the writ and its usages, based on records of the King's Bench, a superior court of the common law, and which oversaw civil corporations, but also covered the criminal and the crown side of judiciary. Crucially it protected the remedy of the subject – and that phrase reminds all concerned that they were the king's or queen's subjects who stood in the dock.

Halliday records that in the 3 centuries of his survey, 2,757 prisoners used habeas corpus and that 'basic multiplication suggests that at least 11,000 people … resorted to the writ … although the actual number was probably much greater'. Halliday looks at underlying modes of judgement '… that a judge should hear the sighs of all prisoners, regardless of where, how, or by whom they were held'. My earlier survey of the multiplicity of courts across Tudor Britain makes it plain that local justice was a long way from the central courts in London, and on a lower scale, the sentences meted out by magistrates and church courts, manorial courts and others, was similarly a long way from the periodic assizes run by the travelling justices. The result of this was that a very large number of people would have been tried and sentenced to a prison stretch, and the idea of anyone issuing a writ of habeas corpus to have the body of the convicted taken to a higher court, or the perpetrator of an abuse taken to be tried was never in consideration. But there were exceptions, and Paul Halliday begins his book with the case of one Walter Wytherley, who had been tried and convicted by the Council of the Marches in Wales. His offence was to face the Council over property ownership, and he had been jailed and forgotten. As Halliday puts it, he 'suffered terribly, drinking his own urine by the time his ordeal ended'.

But somehow, Wytherley had organised a writ of habeas corpus to be sent to the King's Bench, requesting that court to investigate his gaoler, Francis Hunnyngs. Poor Wytherly had been very sorely and harshly treated, having been confined in what was known as 'the little ease' – a tight confinement in isolation. Now he was released, and proceedings began against Hunnyngs, who argued that he was doing the king's business. This was in 1605, and he referred to James I. The Council of the Marches was an extension of the Privy Council itself; therefore influence, inside knowledge and local power structures would have all played a part in this instance. But justice was done. Halliday concludes that: 'Witherley had not confronted the King; rather he took the King's name in his own cause … His was a silent role, played in the opening scenes that set in motion the main events: a struggle between two great courts …'

By 1679 legislation was passed that spelled out very clearly what was wrong in the legal machinery of dealing with abusive, inhumane or wrong-headed penal treatment. The wording of the Habeas Corpus Amendment Act of that year even dealt with practicalities of serving and overseeing the production of the writ:

> That whensoever any person or persons shall bring any habeas corpus directed unto any sheriff or sheriff's gaoler, minister or other person whatsoever or any person in his or her custody and the said writ shall be served upon the said officer or left at the gate of the prison with any of the underofficers …

The Act specified that the writ had to lead to the person concerned being at the court within three days. The lists of paragraphs in the Act make it clear that the producers of the legislation are well informed about where abuses may occur, such as tricks that could be used to cause delays in the process. If this is compared with the notion of habeas corpus under the Tudors, what strikes the historian is that the writ seems only to have existed on the other side of justice – the application of punishment. Paul Halliday gives a perfect example: '… in 1554, Queen's Bench used two writs to bring ninety-seven of Thomas Wyatt's companions to trial for their rebellion … In the margin of the enrolled copies of their writs we can still read the clerk's simple notes that they should hang.' Such was the tyranny of the Marian years, when the concept of individual persons and related rights to a fair trial were not in the vocabulary of the applied law.

In the relentless progress of religious uniformity, naturally there were spin-off problems, and once again, some thought on the justices in the shires and parishes reminds us that in a world in which heresy was so feared, there would be not only underground debates on what were unacceptable desired norms of behaviour, but also on what were alternative paths to the spiritual satisfactions of such matters as the Lutheran precepts of the soul and its relationships to God. What place was there for an individual's meaningful thinking about the major issues of morality and spiritual belief in the Bible and other writings. Luther wanted the Bible in the vernacular; through Christendom and the Catholic focus on Christ himself, Latin had been the linguistic medium for worship; now there was a realisation that scriptures in the language spoken in streets, in the villages and in the fields, were desirable. This would shatter the sheer mystique of the priesthood and the established understanding that the genuine thinking should be done by the elite while the common folk could concentrate on doing Godly things such as hard graft and obedience to the church law, with its roots in Roman law, and expressed through ecclesiastical courts.

What stood outside of all this establishment was the individual thinker, and here the law stepped in, because free thinking could mean trouble in the natural hierarchy of the chain of being. Before

Mary, back in the 1520s, a figure emerged who would be at first an eccentric, and in the end, a perceived danger. This was Elizabeth Barton, known most generally as 'The Holy Maid of Kent', who was born in 1506 and began, as so many young women did, in service. But abnormalities in her physiology, extending to paralysis and desperate life-threatening illness, mixed with visions; these became, she announced, divine revelations. In a Protestant world she spread the need to be a Catholic, and she later became known as a 'Holy Maid'. In this we find similarities to such later phenomena as the mysterious and sometimes saintly fasting girls across the land. In the years between *c.*1800 and the 1870s these figures became fascinating to the general population, and their impact in terms of religious devotion and approaches to prayer and spirituality or worship had a wide impact. Elizabeth's influence developed in a similar way; there was a backing to her growing insistence on prophecies, even from the notable figure of William Warham, the Archbishop of Canterbury.

Such things as visions and revelations had to be checked out. People were seeing her as something more than a maid and a colourful character with strange insights and pronouncements. After an investigation by Edward Bocking, an influential churchman close to Warham and trusted by him, Elizabeth's star rose even further. There was even a healing, done before the country folk of Lympne in Kent. This kind of thing tended to open up interest among those with power, and it surely was no surprise to many when her notoriety was at such widespread proportions that she might be a challenge to orthodoxy, and that challenge could easily be political. Henry VIII and advisers saw all this. In 1532 the Holy Maid made declarations about the dangers involved in the king's attempts to annul his marriage to Catherine of Aragon. This would have been dangerous ground for the average ascendant radical, but for a woman with such a following it was asking for serious trouble. Rather than a measure of sheer forced suppression, the king's men began a campaign of eating away at her status and reputation. But this was not extreme enough.

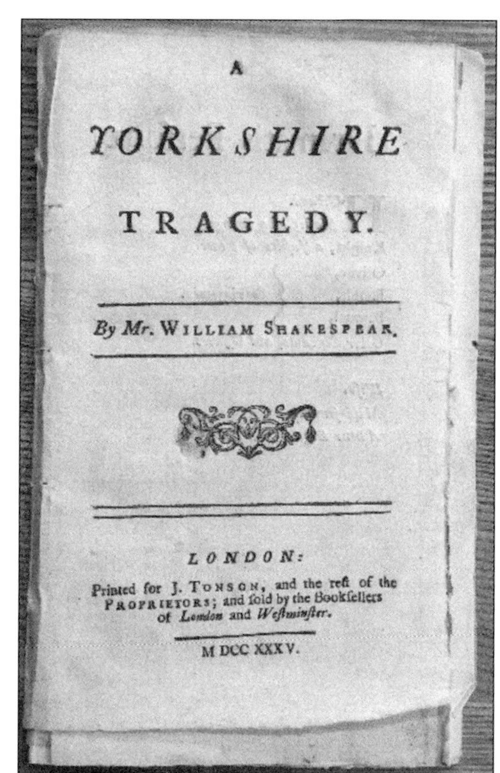
A

YORKSHIRE

TRAGEDY.

By Mr. WILLIAM SHAKESPEAR.

LONDON:

Printed for J. TONSON, and the reſt of the PROPRIETORS; and ſold by the Bookſellers of *London* and *Weſtminſter*.

M DCC XXXV.

Right: An eighteenth-century edition of *A Yorkshire Tragedy*, attributed to Shakespeare. (Author)

Below: One of a series of pictures illustrating Joseph Hirst's *The Blockhouses of Hull* (1913).

THE DVETIES
OF
Conſtables, Borſholders,
Tythingmen, and ſuch o-
ther lowe and Lay Mini-
ſters of the Peace.
Whereunto be adioyned, the ſe-
uerall offices of Church Miniſters
and Churchwardens, and Ouerſeers
for the Poore, Surueighours of the
highwaies, and diſtributors
of the prouiſion againſt
noyſome fowle and
vermine.
Firſt collected by WILLIAM LAMBARD
of Lincolnes Inne Gent. 1582,
and now enlarged by him
in the yeare 1599.

LONDON
Printed by Thomas Wight, and
Bonham Norton, 1599.
Cum Priuilegio Regiæ Maieſtatis.

Above: An old print showing the death by pressing of Saint Margaret Clitherow of York. (Author)

Left: One of many printed guides for officers working in local justice. Similar manuals were also written for the overworked justices. (Author)

THE

REPORTS

OF

Sir Edward Coke, K^{t}.

LATE

Lord Chief Justice

OF

ENGLAND.

OF

Divers Reſolutions and Judgments given upon ſolemn Arguments, and with great Deliberation, and Conference of the moſt Reverend Judges, and Sages of the LAW; of Caſes in Law which never were Reſolved or Adjudged before; And the Reaſons and Cauſes of the ſaid Reſolutions and Judgments.

The Second Edition carefully Compared with the French, *and purged from former Errors.*

With a TABLE to the Whole.

LONDON,

Printed for *H. Twyford*, *T. Collins*, *T. Baſſet*, *J. Wright*, *S. Heyrick*, *T. Sawbridge*, *M. Pitt*, *C. Harper*, and *J. Place*. MDCLXXX.

Sir Edward Coke's *Reports*, still an influential law book. It gives common law and court trial material on cases. (Author)

From Hirst's book on blockhouses, another terrifying image of persecution.

One of the hundreds of ecclesiastical institutions that fell victim to Henry VIII's dissolution of the monasteries in the 1530s. (*Old Yorkshire*, 1888)

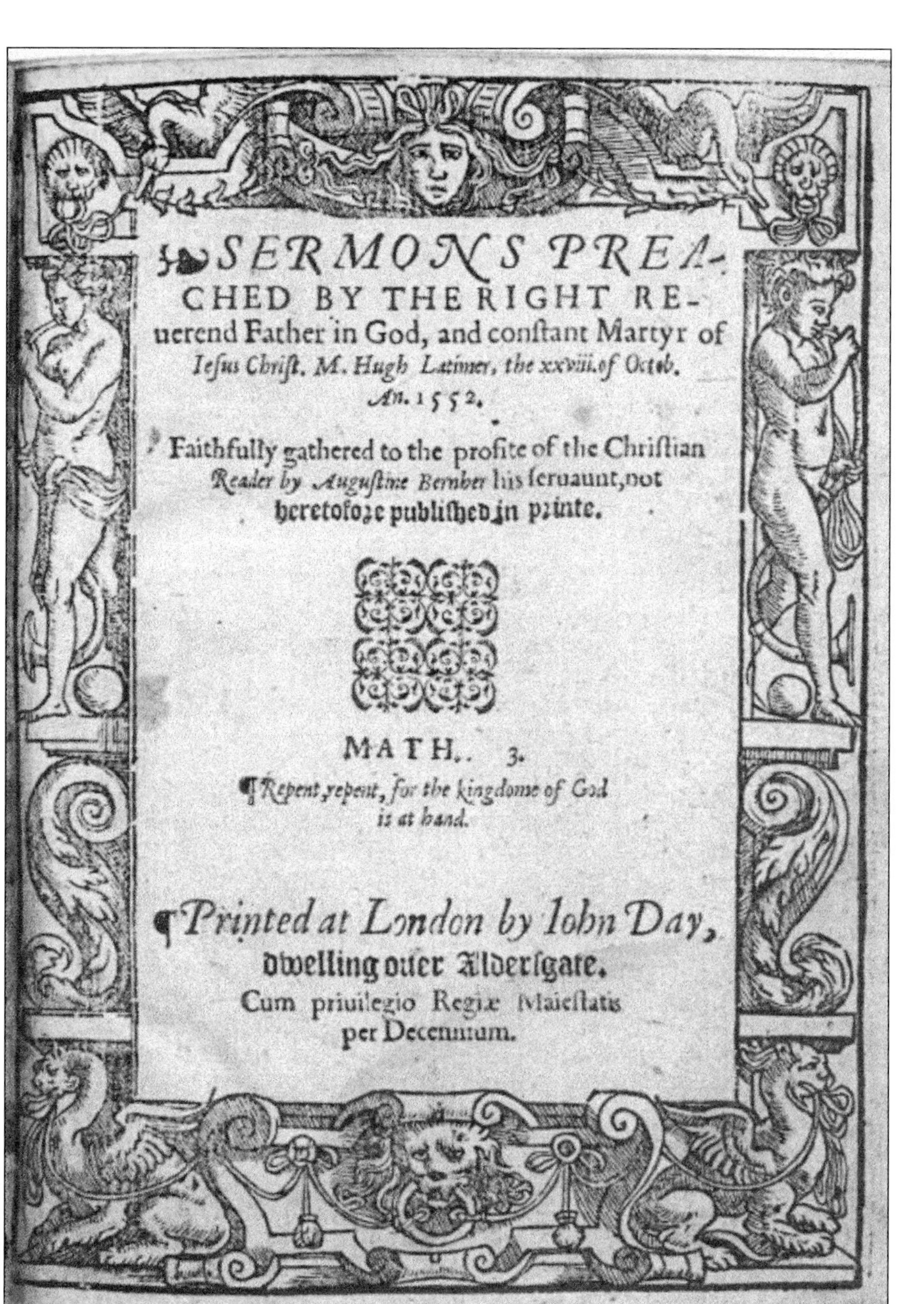

SERMONS PREA-
CHED BY THE RIGHT RE-
uerend Father in God, and conſtant Martyr of
Ieſus Chriſt. M. Hugh Latimer, the xxviii. of Octob.
An. 1552.

Faithfully gathered to the profite of the Chriſtian
Reader by Auguſtine Bernher his ſeruaunt, not
heretofore publiſhed in printe.

MATH. 3.

¶*Repent, repent, for the kingdome of God*
is at hand.

¶*Printed at London by Iohn Day,*
dwelling ouer Alderſgate.
Cum priuilegio Regiæ Maieſtatis
per Decennium.

An edition of *Sermons* by Hugh Latimer, 1571. He was burned at Oxford in 1555. (Author)

Another ghastly image from Hirst's book on blockhouses. (Author)

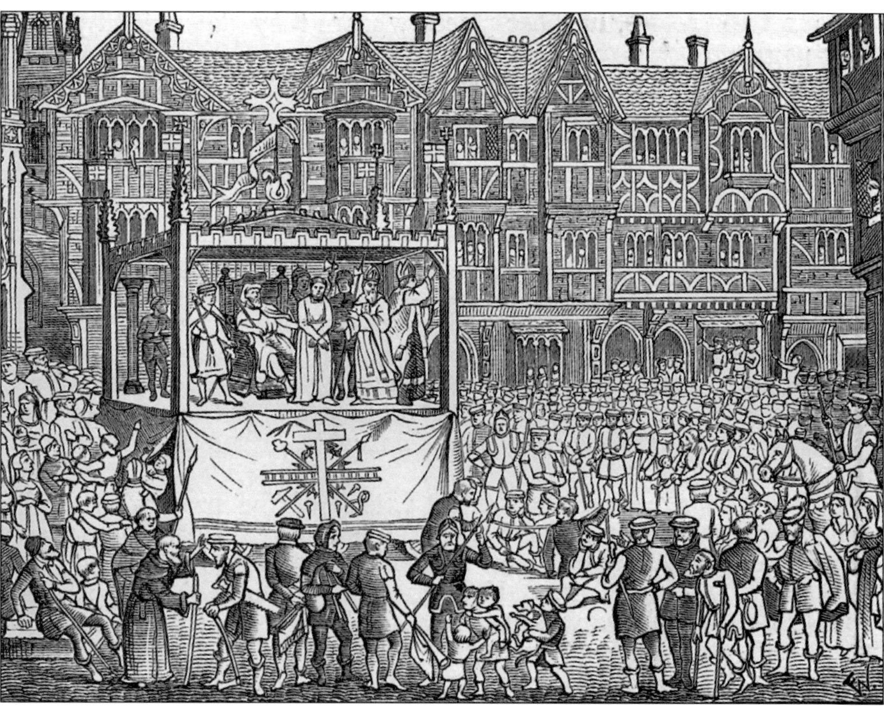

An old print of a morality play. Such occasions were ideal hunting grounds for pickpockets. (*Old Yorkshire* magazine, 1881, author)

A mass hanging during the heresy persecutions, from a Victorian print. (Author)

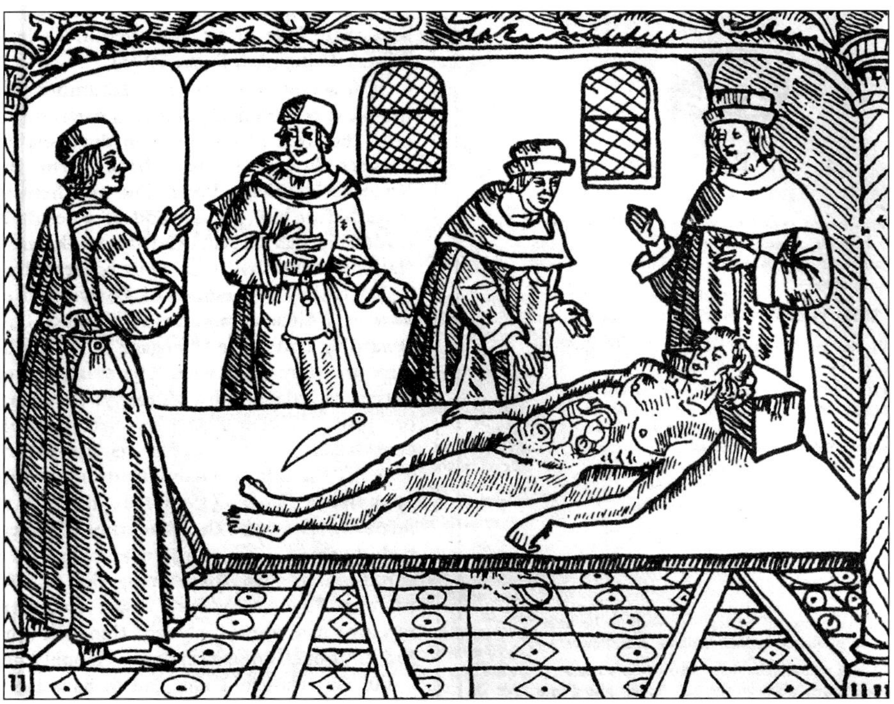

From a book on Renaissance medicine, this shows the work in progress in a drawing of an autopsy. Famously, Rembrandt painted a scene of such a demonstration.

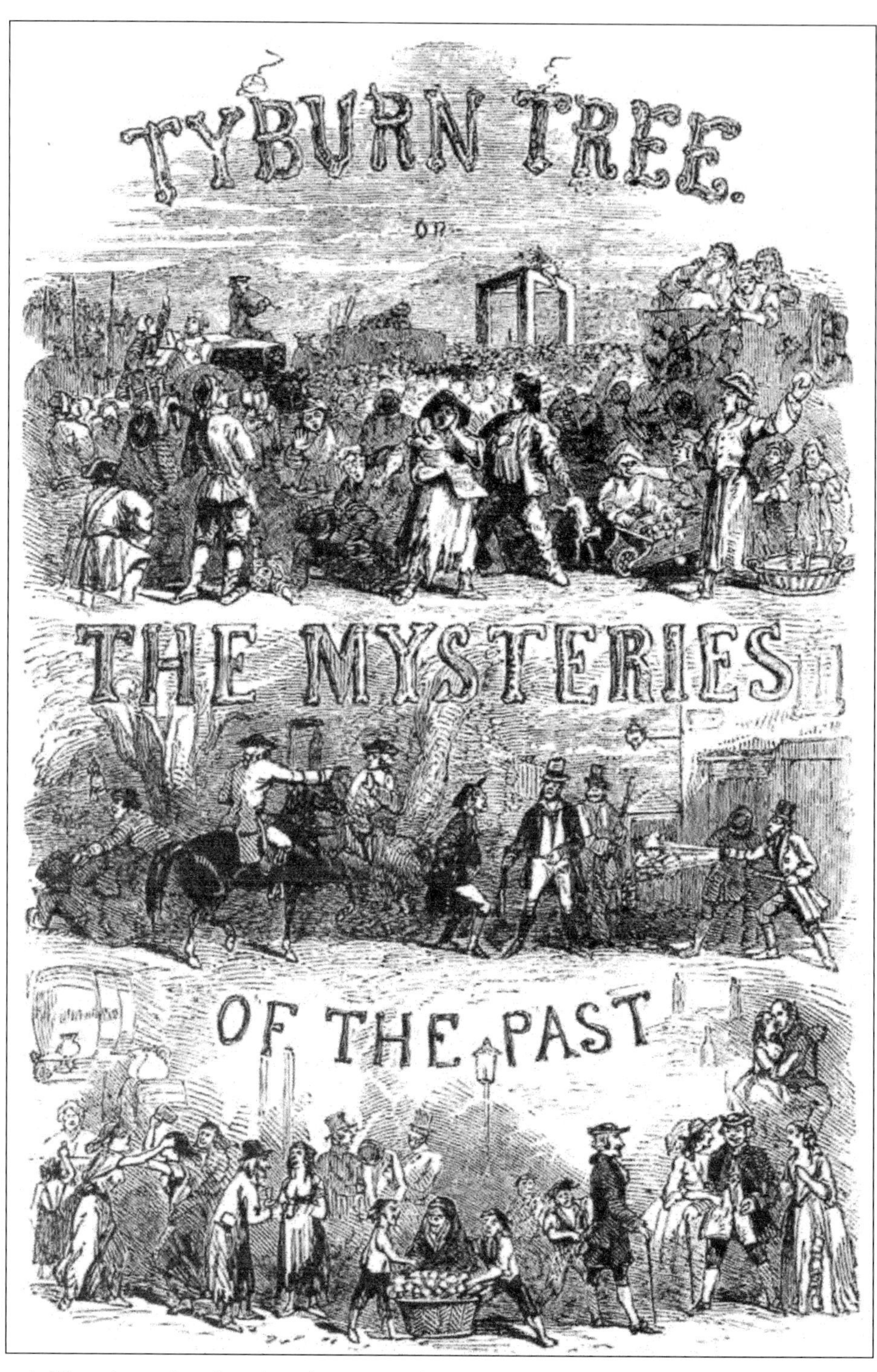

A Victorian print showing the scenes from the history of the prison. It was first mentioned in 1188 and became the gaol supplying the London Tyburn for hangings. (Author)

Right: A picture of the famous Knaresborough future predictor – in stereotype witch apparel. (Author)

Below: A drawing from a Victorian booklet by the printer Ritchie *c*.1880. (Author)

A drawing of a priory, a common punishment for minor offences though serious injuries often resulted in its use. (*Old Yorkshire*, 1888)

A print of the York Minster from 1862. Note the small prison by the side, on the right. (*Annals of Yorkshire*, 1870)

Right: A drawing from a chapbook of the eighteenth century showing the familiar features of a supposed witch. (Author)

Below: One of the most heartrending images from Hirst's book on blockhouses, showing the plight of priests trying to escape pursuit and certain death.

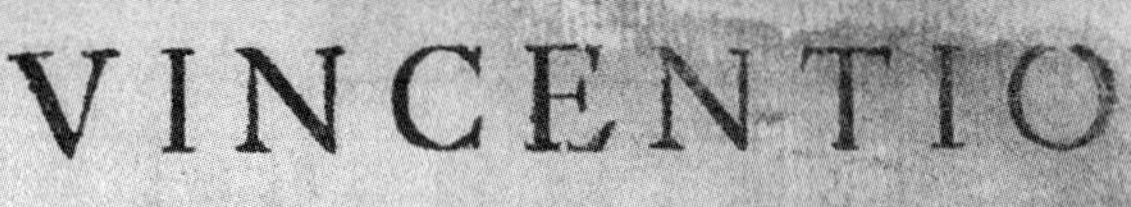

VINCENTIO

SAVIOLO

his Practiſe.

In two Bookes.

The firſt intreating of the vſe of the Rapier and Dagger.

The ſecond, of Honor and honorable Quarrels.

LONDON

Printed by IOHN WOLFE.

1595.

Left: Vincentio Saviolo's popular handbook on fencing – essential for a Tudor rake wanting to settle a matter of honour. (Author)

Below and opposite: Another two images of local punishment for small crimes – brutal and extreme, of course, but expected in the Tudor world. (*Old Yorkshire*, 1888)

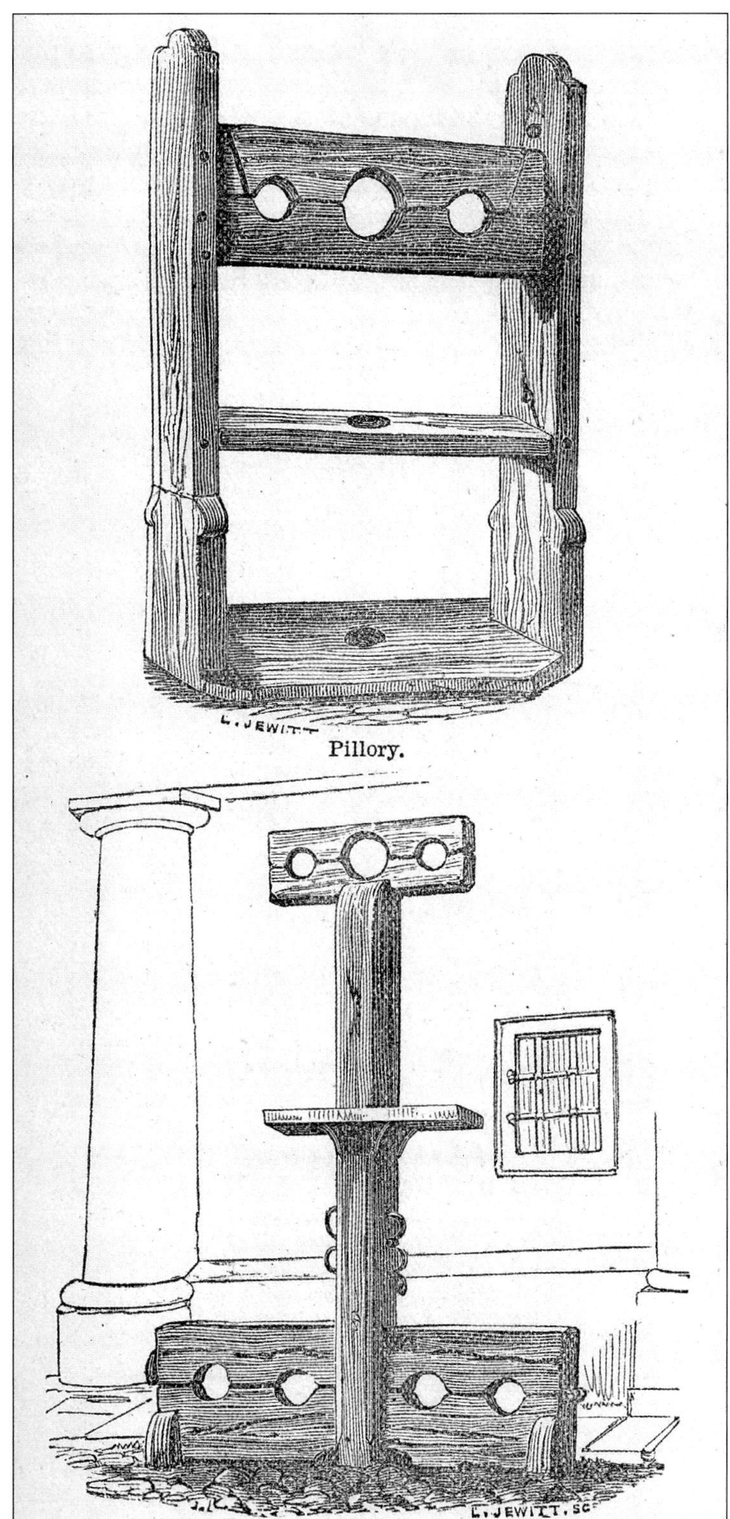

Pillory.

The place where the litigious John Parkins was imprisoned in the 1530s monthly supplement of the *Penny Magazine*, 1835. (Author)

An image of a beheading from 1552, *The New Popular Educator*, 1880. (Author)

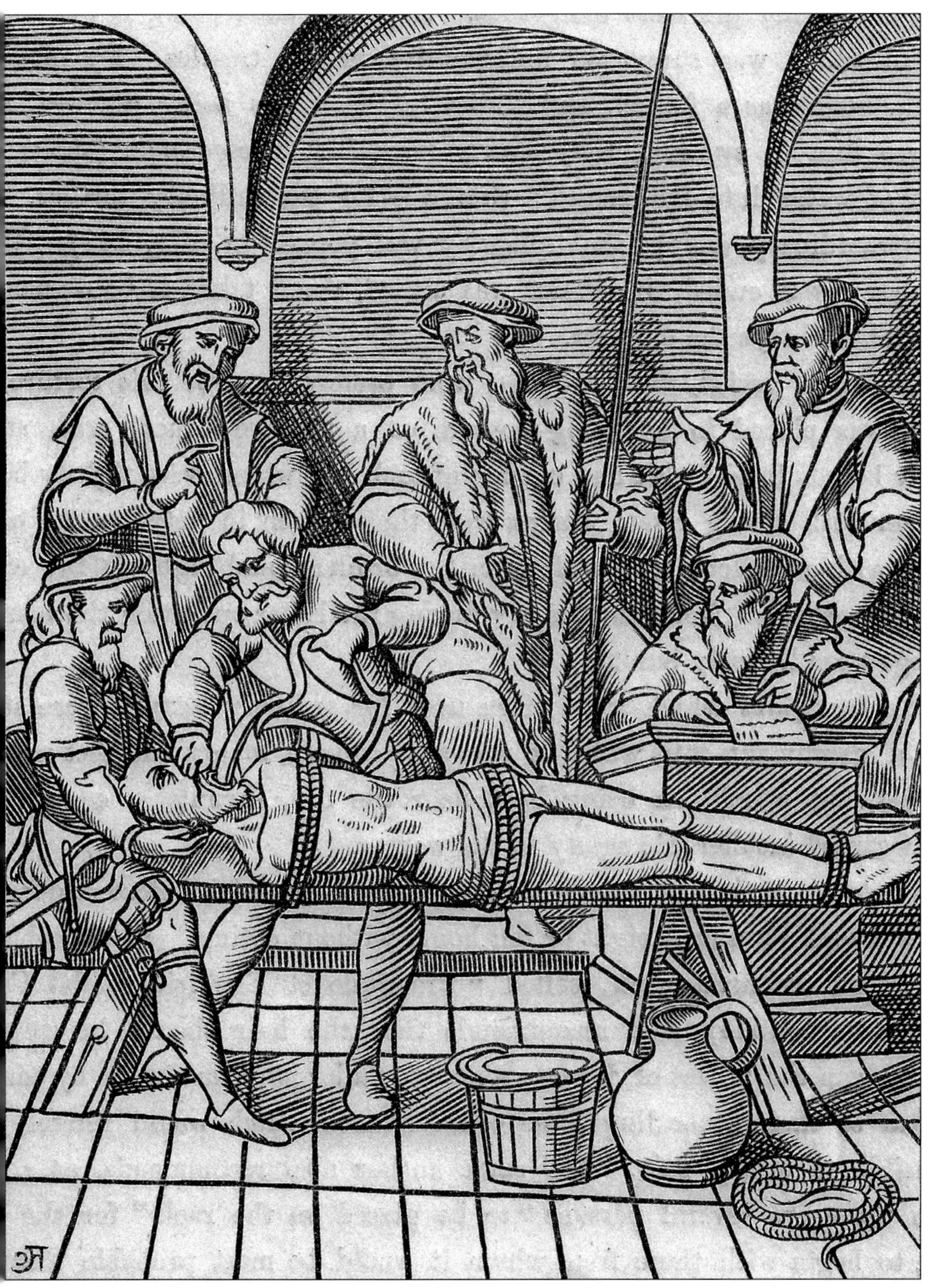

A revolting scene from a woodcut image of 1556 – *Praxis Rerum Criminalium.* (Author)

An axe and block from the Tower of London. (Younghusband, *The Tower of London*)

She was arrested in 1533. The friars around her turned against her and gave evidence that led to an attainder, which has survived as the 1533 Pretended Revelations Act. One has to reflect on this measure. The Henrician world was becoming increasingly like a bizarre microcosm of surreal madness in which if a person belched there might be a statute against belching on the books by the end of the week. This Revelations Act made it possible to have Elizabeth or any other pretender to visions liable to direct punishment, bypassing the court. Where was habeas corpus here, we have to ask? The attainder concept is defined as: 'When a person was convicted of treason or felony he was sentenced to death for the same, or when judgement for outlawry for treason or felony was pronounced against anyone he was said to be tainted' (law dictionary definition). The forfeiture of property attached was not abolished until 1870. There are words in the foundation Treason Act of 1351 that apply so well to Barton's case: 'When a man compasses or imagines the death of our lord the king, of our lady his queen …'

Elizabeth had even told the world that God himself did not approve of Henry's reign and what he had done in terms of the church. She was hanged at Tyburn, at only 28, in 1534, along with five priests and friars. She had actually threatened death to the king for his marital inconstancy – something surely no sane person would have attempted. But her threat was from a basis of subversion much more subtle and perhaps perilous to the crown because it came from mania, and that was a condition too risky to deal with leniently.

Care for one's subjects was theoretically part of the sovereign's brief as God's representative on Earth, but in the hierarchical concept of creation as far as Earth was concerned in the cosmic order of things, the king or queen was the one to maintain the required care of the powerless, those who worked daily to preserve the health of the status quo. Crime historians may soon find the obvious weaknesses and shortcomings in the repercussions of the Tudor version of ruler and subjects: they were evident in the gaols. There were to be no general reports or investigations into the conditions in prisons until the groundbreaking work of John Howard in the 1770s and 1780s when he visited gaols across the whole country. One of his overall verdicts on the bridewells at that time was surely something that could have been said in 1600:

> It will perhaps be asked, does not their work maintain them? For everyone knows that these offenders are committed to hard labour. The answer to that question … will hardly be believed. There are few bridewells in which any work is done … The prisoners have neither tools nor materials of any kind, but spend their time in sloth, profaneness and debauchery, to a degree which, in some of those houses that I have seen, are extremely shocking.

One suspects that what happened in the castle gaol of York in 1596 was something that could happen anywhere at any time – a rogue was put in charge of the prison. Here was a man who was eventually confined a prisoner in his own place. The man in question is Robert Redhead, and T.P. Cooper, writing *c.*1900, sums up his wicked deeds in his abuse of power:

> He was overbearing and grasping, and on every possible occasion extorted money from his prisoners. By every subtle pretext he callously and cruelly ill treated those prisoners who were unable to bribe him. His insolent demeanour and defiant attitude towards the Council of the North was a subject of complaint and much correspondence. He evidently amassed a small fortune by his nefarious practices, and was subsequently styled a 'gentleman' and permitted to bear arms …

The Council of the North was, of course, based in York, so the members of that arm of the law and justice at the top level would have had opportunity to watch him and to be aware of his ill doings. Yet he stayed in his position until 1604, when Thomas Beaumont and Michael Clarkson took control. Anyone perusing the state trials of England would soon find prison abuse cases recorded along with related trials, and it is plain from these that similar abuses to those of Redhead were committed in various places, perhaps most notably in the case of John Huggins, warden of the Fleet, who murdered Edward Arne in 1729.

In Scotland, according to Robert Chambers writing in the 1880s, the situation in everyday law was scathing about the situation in 1579 when an Act was passed to try to combat the customary way of conducting legal business: 'An advocate or barrister is spoken of … as taking money from his clients, and dividing it among the judges for their votes. At this time we find the chancellor (Lord Fyvie) superintending the lawsuits of a friend, and writing to him the way and manner in which he proposed they should be conducted.' The Act in question was to stop legal personnel 'by themselves or by their wives and servants to take in any time bribes, goods or articles' and, as Chambers comments, 'Had not bribery been common among the judges such an act of this could never have been passed.'

Robert Southey, friend of Wordsworth and Poet Laureate, wrote of the Devil visiting England in these words:

As he went through Cold Bath Fields he looked
At a solitary cell.
And the Devil was pleased, for it gave him a hint
For improving the prisons of Hell.

Trying to sum up the average Tudor worker in home, field and in any general trade in relation to crime presents the problem of a society pressured to maintain conformity when that shifting definition of obedience and its morality were always blurred. In a world without newspapers, mass media or social interaction beyond tavern and gossip, it is surely valid to suggest that it was a case of people living with full dependence on the church, and more specifically, on the parish priest and the bench of magistrates. These constituted the power they knew and saw regularly. Otherwise, crimes were to be faced and solved mostly on the doorstep, as it were, as in the cases from Kent in my previous chapter.

If we had to find a credit side to this dismal picture, it would be in the fact that although the problem of crime on the highways was not solved, there were fewer rogues and vagabonds around, as the bridewells had absorbed some, and statutes had been stamped and dispatched like a fusillade of bullets in a battle. The only proviso that comes to mind is that a mindset of creating Acts from parliament has the drawback that lawgivers begin to think that curing social ills is simply a matter of passing statutes. It is as if a statute on paper is a completed action, as if an offence is being confronted that is then dealt with. In reality, action was undertaken by the local constables and by the unpaid bench of magistrates. Sooner or later crimes will move from minor irritation to common offence and danger to the realm. Fear drove the Tudor statutes, along with a generous dash of wish fulfilment in the recipe.

Meanwhile, custom still prevailed in the small towns and villages; there were still manors and plenty of legal confrontations, and the common law still had a presence; moreover, the state was part of a greater, enterprising world, and one has to ask what happened to people in the clashes between what was modern and what was acceptable? These questions sat alongside the most dominant challenge of the long reign of Elizabeth (1558–1603) when there was no male successor and Spain wanted to crush and subdue England. There was also the threat of Mary, Queen of Scots and a number of restless aristocrats, to say nothing of a rising Bard of Avon.

As far as the legal battles fought in the courts were concerned, the situation had been, through all the years since Henry VII, a case of a proliferation of courts being used and/or created in order to open up legal action and justice to all the sovereign's subjects. The famous *Reports* of Sir Edward Coke, which are still read and used by lawyers today, balanced common law and its holding place in equity courts, with ranges of other bases of judgement in general cases across the country and with other law sources from statutes to judges. One optimistic element in this situation was that there were opportunities for women to be more of a presence in suits and trials. This was, perhaps, a sign of better things to come.

Chapter 6

Women, Witches and Snitches

Dan Chaucer, the first warbler, whose sweet breath
Precluded those melodious bursts that fill
The spacious times of great Elizabeth.

Tennyson

A metaphor is needed in order to explain something profound in the Elizabethan and early Jacobean years. This is because great, mind-blowing changes were in process and at the root of it was a potent mix of contemporary issues relating to crime and transgression. It is a metaphor of self and transformation.

A Catholic schoolgirl buys a new dress, or is treated to such a garment by parents. It is her first attire outside school uniform. Now, a uniform is about uniformity; it makes one look the same as many others. She puts on the dress, and it is a shiny, golden, charming thing to wear, showing her as a new person, a being suffused with happiness. Looking at herself as she is now, transformed into an individual, the joy rises in her, and along with that feeling come the complexities of being new, feeling like a new creation. Now there are possibilities perhaps, for what had been repressed inside her. In short, what has happened is a revelation of selfhood.

This was the situation of selfhood around this time. It was surely as exciting as a discovery of the New World or of the possibilities of a dizziness of vision and imagination that was widely fusing the rise of natural philosophy, alchemy and the revelations of the astounding particularity of divine creation. It was no accident that in the last years of Elizabeth, Shakespeare was turning towards the thinking behind what scholars call the 'late romances' in which he often depicts a world in transition, a fragile universe that no longer perhaps conforms to the medieval concepts and classical regularity. Into the mouth of Prospero in *The Tempest* he puts these words:

> Our revels now are ended. These our actors as I foretold you, were all spirits and are melted into air, into thin air; and like the baseless fabric of this vision, the cloud-capped towers, the gorgeous palaces, the solemn temples, the great globe itself, yes, all which it inherit, shall dissolve, and like this insubstantial pageant faded, leave not a rack behind …

The great chain of being, together with the ordered hierarchy of the Christian world, the social structures and the moral strictures, this implies, will fall, dissolve, crumble. What emerges from this is a preoccupation of the poets and writers of the time, a theme they called 'mutabilitie'. To put it broadly, here was a state and a population whose grandparents had been taught to see themselves as worms or ants in God's great universe, working and striving for a place in heaven and eternal rest beyond their world of wars, plagues and suffering. Now, here they were thinking about the world across a great sea and lives they could not even imagine.

Women do figure in these trends also. A typical example is that of Mary Sidney, Countess of Pembroke, of Wilton House, Salisbury. Mary had an alchemical laboratory. She was hardly a typical woman of her time, having been raised at Ludlow Castle and having the best education possible at the time. She was multi-lingual, engaged in scientific experiments, and indulged in producing and writing codes. She lived from 1561 to 1621, and had a place in John Aubrey's diaries, in which he wrote that there were many 'learned and ingenious persons' at her home, and that she was '… the greatest patroness of wit and learning of any lady in her time'.

This grand outer world of an unknown Earth and cosmos lay at one end of the spectrum of mind-boggling contemplation, and at the other end was the self, the individual. Richard Davenport-Hines, surveying this idea of the self, writes this, referring to the coming developments in the seventeenth century: 'A line of poetry written by Traherne in 1674 – "a secret self I had enclosed within" – is recorded by the *Oxford English Dictionary* as the first instance in which the word self took its modern meaning of "a permanent subject of successive and varying states of consciousness".' He adds to this an interesting insight with regard to earlier Tudor years:

> Diaries reflected the change in people's awareness of themselves as individuals: a new taste for self-scrutiny becomes discernible. A few diarists of the sixteenth century were not introspective. During the thirteen years after 1550 in which the London undertaker Henry Machyn kept a diary he made only two references to himself: both were to record his birthday, and significantly neither the ages nor the dates tally …

In simple terms, it is arguably an evident trend in the intellectual background to the records of a fair slice of criminal cases that there was a steady disintegration of the kind of community allegiances I discussed in my introduction. The anomie of Durkheim is evident in the literature of the time, together with the tendency of the law to cater for marginal voices. Scholars such as Alexander Shepard and Tim Stretton have analysed the actions and arguments of women in the smaller courts, including the court of requests, to show that there were changes in the law machine as well as in the books, plays and poems.

It is a common trend in the biographies of the literary and intellectual ranks of society to find profiles such as that of Richard Stanyhurst (1547–1618), who translated Virgil but also went through various stages of spiritual interest and experience, 'professing alchemy' at one point, and then eventually took holy orders and was chaplain to the governors of the Netherlands. More prominent figures in Elizabethan years include John Donne, remembered now as a poet but who was also Dean of St Paul's, lawyer and military volunteer.

Relevant to the background of the topic under scrutiny here is the case of Christopher Marlowe, already discussed, and particularly in his play *Dr Faustus.* Here there is a character whose story represents perfectly the search for knowledge, running parallel to the new scientific activities taking place in the study of mankind and nature, and this introduces the other important dimension of these speculations, and something that had a large impact on the law – sorcery, black magic and, most of all, communion with demonic powers. Faustus succumbs to the penalty imposed on those who would push the lust for knowledge too far, and by the imminence of his death, he is torn between the Devil and a God who may yet forgive him: 'See, see where Christ's blood streams in the firmament!/one drop would save my soul –half a drop: ah my Christ!/Ah, rend not my heart for naming of my Christ!/yet will I call on him: oh, spare me, Lucifer.'

Women figure in the other primary interest here as one looks at the crises of fringe activity, forbidden transgressions. Witchcraft and sorcery play a main role here, but before we consider this, a preface is needed, on the subject of women's status in law, and this introduces the fundamental idea of coverture. The law dictionary definition of this term is 'The condition of a wife during her marriage which before the Married Women's Property Acts … involved certain disabilities on the one hand and certain protections or privileges on the other.' (*Mozley and Whiteley's Law Dictionary*). In the language of Lord Wilson in his lecture of 2012, it was something developed in the Norman mindset regarding law, and 'the heart of the new order was reflected in the principle of coverture. In the words of law-French, the wife was a *feme covert* instead of a *feme sole*; in law she was 'covered up by her husband …'

Lord Wilson adds that the wife was 'legally in the shadow of the husband and she was substantially invisible to the law'. The aspect of this that really impacts on women under the Tudors was that wives could not own any property, and her husband could do as he wished with anything she had except for freehold property. What she did acquire after the husband's death was her own chattels – things known as her paraphernalia. Coverture also meant that a wife could not be part of a contract. There was also the serious subject of a wife committing a crime. As Lord Wilson puts it, 'there was one criminal law for the husband and a different one for her'. The most dreadful instance of this gap was in murder and the concept of petit treason. If a husband killed his wife, he had committed murder, but if a wife murdered her husband, the act was equivalent to a servant or subject killing a master, and in the thinking behind this difference, such a husband would be hanged, while a wife would be sentenced to burn at the stake. Petit treason existed until the landmark legislation of the 1861 Offences Against the Person Act.

A classic case of petit treason rooted in wife and lover working together is in the death of John Cotell at Farleigh Castle in 1522. Cotell's wife, Agnes, was involved with this, and a feature on the History of Parliament site by Dr Simon Payling explains what happened to Agnes:

> Her indictment in the following August was followed by her conviction in Hilary term 1523 and she was hanged at Tyburn. Fortunately for her, she was spared burning. As she had been indicted as an accessory, she could not be convicted of a greater offence than the principals, and since they had been convicted of murder, she could not be convicted of petit treason. The irony was that, had the murderers been described in the indictment as servants of the victim, she would not have enjoyed that limited protection.

Decades before these crises of faith and excitements of new and forbidden knowledge, there was the advent of witchcraft, and this plays a major role in the long and desperately negative chronicle of the place of women in the scheme of things regarding crime, law and justice for the Tudors. In his historical span of time and reference in his 1841 work *Extraordinary Popular Delusions and the Madness of Crowds*, Charles Mackay covers the basic background of the growth of witchcraft in Early Modern Europe generally. The title here perhaps suggests a tone of exaggeration, but Mackay does produce such alarming statistics of cases and punishments for witchcraft that conclusions about the range and intensity of prosecutions are staggering. Mackay states:

> Upon a very moderate calculation, it is presumed that from the passing of the act of Queen Mary till the accession of James I to the throne of England, a period of thirty-nine years, the average number of executions for witchcraft in Scotland was two hundred annually, or upwards of seventeen thousand altogether. For the first nine years the number was not one quarter so great, but towards the years 1590 to 1593, the number must have been more than four hundred.

A general definition of witchcraft as understood then, without modern refinements of range and application, might be one stated *c.*1930: 'The supposed art of producing supernatural effects of a malignant nature by the agency of evil spirits.' There were fundamental events and actions in the European background, and most significant of these was a papal bull issued from Pope Innocent VIII. In this he asked everyone in the realms of Christendom 'imperilled by the arts of Satan, and set forth the horrors that had reached his ears; how that numbers of both sexes had been having intercourse with the infernal fiends; how by their sorceries they inflicted both man and beasts …'

By 1541 Henry VIII's parliament issued a Witchcraft Act, and from then on this became a felony at law, which means essentially that a guilty person would die and he would lose his property to the crown. The benefit of clergy was removed from the advent of trial and pleading, and it may be seen in the explanations of what it was intended to suppress and punish exactly what the fears were. The primary offence was to 'use, devise, practise or exercise any … invocations or conjurations of spirits, witchcrafts, enchantments or sorceries' and added to these was the intent to 'waste, consume or destroy any person in his body members'. Added to this was the more dramatic and frightening wording of, 'Or … dig up or pull down any cross or crosses or by such invocations … take upon them to declare where goods stolen or lost shall become …'

In 1562, there was a revision, as the previous Act was abolished in 1547. There was now death if harm was ascertained by actions of witchcraft and sorcery. There were incarceration options too, not necessarily the death penalty. In practice there was a fairly high rate of acquittals. In Scotland, an Act of the following year made witchcraft or any person working with or speaking with a witch subject to the death penalty.

The extent and impact of witchcraft cases and reports may be gauged from the fact that Bishop Jewell, when he gave sermons to Elizabeth I, as Mackay reports, '… used constantly to conclude them with a fervent prayer that she might be preserved from witches'. He described the effects of such sorcery in words which give us a clear idea of how these offences were reported: 'Your grace's subjects pine away even unto the death; their colour fadeth – their flesh rotteth – their speech is benumbed – their senses are bereft! I pray God they may never practise further than upon the subject!'

If case studies are needed to understand how accusations of witchcraft happened and what the consequences were, we need look no further than the story of the Samuel family or Warbois in Huntingdon, and this narrative illustrates the nature of a moral panic and indeed an epidemic of alleged crime and irrational accusation. The basic logistical problem here is that during these years, a crazed and unfounded accusation could arise from trivia, from invented actions and from hysterical attitudes.

Warboys, as it is spelled today, extends back to a Saxon charter of 974, and it probably does not particularly want to be remembered as the place where one of the most popularised and examined witchcraft cases in English history is situated. The story concerns the Samuel family, and it began with an episode that has a character now very common in the legends and chronicles of witchcraft – the pointing of accusation (and following criminal charges) of an old woman in a small, seemingly stable community. The history and the legendary elements of witchcraft as a crime and as a social trend is now cluttered with incident, strong human stories and utter revulsion. As I will examine in the following pages with a focus on Scotland, it can be seen as a subject bound up also with inhumanity, torture and extreme suffering, often in a mix of half-truth, sick imagination and local enmity, reaching from ordinary village life up to the court of James I and VI (of Scotland).

The Samuel family's ordeals began when Joan Throgmorton, walking in the village, saw Mother Samuel knitting, and Joan, in the words of Charles Mackay '… immediately fancied that she felt sudden pains in all her limbs, and from that day forth never ceased to tell her sisters, and everybody about her, that Mother Samuel had bewitched her'. The course of events around Warbois after that reads like some kind of cheap, far-fetched oral traditional tale, or a yarn from a bad dream. To a modern reader, it could be a bundle of popular narrative tropes from the worst kind of cartoon or B movie. But one has to pause, and reflect that the kind of alleged behaviour in the story promulgated by the locals, Lady Cromwell and Mrs Throgmorton is outlined by Charles Mackay:

> Seven spirits, they said, were raised from hell by this wicked woman to throw them into fits; and as the

> children were actually subject to fits, the mother and her commeres gave the more credit to the story. The names of these spirits were First Smack, Second Smack, Third Smack, Blue, Catch, Hardname and Pluck.

The persecution of Mother Samuel and her family continued for over a year. Naturally, the neighbourhood in general believed the tales. The attitudes hardened into bullying and forced actions by Sir Samuel Cromwell, and on one occasion Mother Samuel was in a situation described by Mackay that actually delineates a puppet-like response to commands:

> Being forcibly brought into Mr Throgmorton's house, when his daughter Jean was in one of her customary fits, she was commanded by him and Sir Samuel Cromwell to expel the devil from the young lady. She was told to repeat her exorcism and to add, 'As I am a witch, and the causer of Lady Cromwell's death, I charge thee, fiend, to come out of her!' She did as was required of her and moreover confessed that her husband and daughter were leagued with her in witchcraft and had, like her, sold their souls to the devil.

The inevitable happened: the Samuels were interrogated and tortured. One of the truly revolting sides of this business comes out when we recall that at this time the thumbscrew, known also as the pilly-winks, was used. In the later Scottish witch cases, as will be shown later in the chapter, Ailson Balfour was tortured to elicit a confession. Her son was whipped, and she had the pilly-winks applied. Images of these horrendous tools of torture show their use: three vertical rods have one lateral bar across them, and one or two solid screws are placed on one or more of the rods. It is obvious, from a moment's reflection, how easy it would be with these devices to break finger bones.

Torture did not sit easily in notions of punishment when it came to the church, as Blessin Adams showed in her treatment of the Richard Hunne case, discussed in the previous chapter, but in the witch narratives, there were few restraints in this respect.

In the Warbois story, the Samuels were hanged in April 1593. Sir Samuel Cromwell gained £40 from the Samuels' property taken after the trial, as they had, of course, committed a felony.

A look at witchcraft trials in Scotland cannot be avoided in this context, and matters in this instance are very much intensified when one reflects that James I and VI was himself not only the author of a book on the subject, but was, in his mind, a victim of sorcery. James married Anne of Denmark, and after they came back home from their wedding, James insisted that a storm at sea when Anne was aboard ship was raised by witches. A storm hit him again when returning from Denmark, and again he blamed witchcraft. Witches were found in North Berwick, and there was no room for studying the meteorology of the circumstances. His mind saw sorcery at work, and not only were the dark arts blamed, but confessions were taken. Six so-called witches were executed, and as Magnus Magnusson wrote, '… it was the start of a horrifying witch-hunt which over the next century would claim more than a thousand victims, 80 per cent of whom were women'.

James' book was *Daemonologie*, published in 1597. It obviously had a notable impact on society and was reprinted in 1603. It is a work in dialogue form, and explains sorcery and the workings of demons, particularly dealing with how demons are alleged to work their dark designs on mankind; the trials in North Berwick, and makes the case for the practices of witch-hunting that were beginning. James was convinced that what he called 'assaults of Satan were happening', and in a world in which such witch hunting had been absorbed into the workings of criminal justice and state authority, he patently thought the general public needed some instruction on the subjects he thought were clearly seen in the events behind the witch trials.

He was convinced that what he called the 'detestable slaves of the Devil', the witches or enchanters, needed to be interpreted and explained to his subjects.

There were plenty of other prominent witch trials in Scottish history during the Tudor years, and not all of these concerned female accused. Examples are Sir Lewis Ballantyne, who was supposedly in communication with a warlock called Richard Grahame. But one case stands out as being notably the story of Gellie Duncan and Dr Fian in 1591. Duncan was from Tranent, near Edinburgh, and like so many accused of witchcraft, she claimed that her activities had a purpose of healing. The problem with this, back in these times of superstition and very limited knowledge of medical science, was that so-called cures could cross the boundaries of common sense and common practice into something so radical that it stirred accusations of unnatural practices.

Once again, Charles Mackay describes what happened once torture had succeeded accusation:

> … the worthy bailiff … mistrusted her and considered them [her healing methods] no less than miraculous. In order to discover the truth, he put her to the torture; but she obstinately refused to confess that she had dealings with the Devil. It was the popular belief that no witch could confess as long as the marks which Satan had put upon her remained undiscovered upon her body. Somebody present reminded the bailie of this fact … and the Devil's mark was found upon the throat of poor Gellie.

Dr Fian had been a teacher at Tranent, and he was also tortured, with a group of others; he was put on the rack, which was a frame that stretched the limbs and joints for the purpose of inflicting extreme agony. His treatment provides one of the worst examples of the use of torture in this context. He experienced the horrors of his fingernails being forced out, and then he was put in the 'Boots'. The aim was to elicit a forced confession. The Boots was an application of a wooden frame to a leg or elsewhere, tightly placed on the limb, so that other wedges could be driven into the small space and inflict great pain on the subject. Fian gave a forced confession, but then retracted. He was booted again, and one old account of Fian's suffering notes, '... so long, and abode so many bows in them, that his legs were crushed and beaten together as small as might be, and the bones and flesh so bruised that the blood and marrow spouted forth in great abundance, whereby they were made unserviceable for ever'.

Some of the case studies of witches show clear instances of young women who had strong imaginations combined with straitened circumstances and itinerant lives – foundations for exploitation and victimisation. This is evidently seen in the story of Elspeth Reoch, who was born in Caithness and broadcast her ability to use magic abilities. The point about her situation is that in Orkney there were old-established attitudes to whatever 'magical powers' could be defined as. When Elspeth claimed to have them, the land of Orkney in her time was ruled by Patrick Stewart, 2nd Earl of that land, but he was deposed and James I placed James Law, Bishop of Orkney there. Elspeth was noticed and thought to be an offender. She was probably only a deluded child, but she was questioned.

She claimed that two strangers had approached her and said that they could give her extraordinary powers; after a while, there was Elspeth with an infant, and she said that she had been intimate with a figure she called 'the fairie man'. Under questioning, the poor girl spoke of all this, and the words used were changed, placing her well under the shadow of the accusatory wording of the Witchcraft Act. It shakes the twenty-first century sensibility like a sapling in a blizzard to think that this little girl was defined as a witch and was strangled to death before her remains were destroyed. All this was happening at the time when the age of savagery and cruelty should have been something outside the law, but the revulsion is there in every word of the record relating to Elspeth Reoch. It is a tale that opens up the barbarism that can hide under a cloak of justice.

As popular history and the media have made well known, the occupation of witch finder became a feature of the subculture around this area of the law. The later witch finders of Essex have stolen the limelight here but the finders, or 'pickers' as they were sometimes known, have their own stories. Mackay accounts for one activity of these questionable experts in searching out the dark arts deviants: 'It was no unusual thing … that in aged persons there should be some spot on the body devoid of feeling. It was the object of the witch-pricker to discover this spot, and the unhappy wight who did not bleed when pricked upon it was doomed to death.'

In the years of James, the first Stuart, witchcraft prosecutions carried on through to the years just after the Civil Wars. It was not until 1721 that the records show the last person in England to be hanged. This was Jane Wenham at Hereford. In 1775 the last witch to be executed as a witch in the whole of Europe was Anna Schwagel in Bavaria.

It is greatly significant that in folklore studies and popular cultural reference, folk tales and legends, tales of witches, either in criminal records or in the imaginations of writers, have featured prominently. Katherine Briggs, the specialist in folk tales and folklore, wrote in her preface to a collection of these stories: 'The study of industrial folklore and of the traditional customs are obviously of importance to sociologists, as are expressions of Mob Psychology, witch hunts of all periods, and racial prejudice.' The reference here is to the accumulation of witch narratives across cultures over the centuries, and the Tudor and Stuart years have the foundation cases embedded in them, from children's tales to Arthur Miller's play *The Crucible* of 1953.

Women and the law is a theme that opens up more questions than answers, but the topic of coverture discussed earlier in the chapter explains the general context. To understand actual illustrations of their obstacles and sufferings at the hands of the male-centre culture that was the Tudor establishment and governance, there is a need to show the picture through human stories.

In the case of my ongoing account of everyday law, the locations of these stories are in the courts, in the issues around wards, and some individual accounts of outstanding women. Some of these I will reserve to the following chapter because in a world of religion-related crimes, women figured prominently. For the everyday stories, the Star Chamber courts and the court of requests offer up some enlightening tales.

Tim Stretton's work on women in the Tudor courts, *Women Waging War in Elizabethan England*, focuses mainly on the court of requests, and although this court has been mentioned briefly earlier, it needs to be used again here in order to clarify women's place in the legal process. Stretton shows that around 20 per cent of plaintiffs in the court of requests were women, and his material is largely cultural in order to answer the questions raised by the facts. In his review of Stretton's book, Daniel Klerman highlights a principal issue: 'Stretton shows that women were also discouraged from litigating by the idea that a modest woman speaks little, that a chaste woman does not appear in public, and that a good woman is ignorant of her rights.' All this makes sense, and obviously prompts the reader to think again about *The Merchant of Venice*, in which play Portia, acting as lawyer against Shylock, has these words:

> The world is still deceived with ornament. In law, what plea so tainted and corrupt but, being seasoned with a gracious voice, obscures the show of evil?

Thinking about the implications in this comment on people facing legal professionals in a law suit, the nature of the court of requests needs to be stressed. It was conceived in the reign of Richard III, and it was probably dropped and then later resumed 'into its normal functioning of the king's council its activity in hearing the suits of poor persons which had been separated by Richard III' as Hannes Kleineke puts it. Kleineke confirms the court's purpose and writes of its 'specific responsibility for hearing the petitions of those seeking justice directly from the king, especially those too poor to have access to the normal remedies of the common law …' From the 1530s it was established in Westminster, and one can imagine the female litigants needed their Portias.

A similar situation was the case with another major topic in this world ruled by coverture: the concept of wardships. As so often with Henry VIII, this was all about making money. At school, my history teacher used to make up rhymes to aid learning, and for the Tudors he had this:

> Build a palace, and feel pleasant;
> don't think about the starving peasant.
> Keep your treasure under key and lock,
> and send your enemies to the block.

There is no doubt that the system again had its own court – the court of wards and liveries. This was created by Henry VIII in two statutes of 1540 and 1541 and was undoubtedly about money and profit. The business of wards was concerned with those orphans who were heirs to estates. Wardship was a royal prerogative, in a feudal context, and was a part of the nature of guardianship. Wards and their guardians figure in a great deal of later literature, and the fact that a young female ward was potentially a lucrative 'catch' for a young man in search of an easy fortune means stories of this kind figured in comedies as much as in sad tales of abduction.

The 1535 Statute of Usages made sure that there was royal profit in wardships. Basically, in the case of the estate of a dead person, any wardship would be there to be sold by the king to whoever offered the price he wanted. It was something as profitable as the use and gifts relating to sinecures, and was part of elaborate systems of transactions in which a young heir or heiress was like a human commodity. There was a concept of *seisin in deed*, which is when a feudal possession is taken. There had to be a gathering for inquisition when a tenant died, deciding rents and obligations. This was registered in the court of wards. On the arrival of the Tudors and Henry VII this area of manorial life was obviously seen as a very good source of income. In the early years of Henry VIII, investigators were at work checking on cases involving crown land that would and could arise anywhere. The process needed a supervisor, and so the office of Master of the King's Wards was made. A steady cash source was established.

These offices and duties provide a perfect example of the workings of the Tudor court, with the sovereign at the centre and circles of status and influence around them; so specific places and duties could be brought and applied as rewards or indeed sometimes as demotions in that world of favouritism and esteem. A fall from position, and from 'grace' in language almost seeing the monarch as demigod, is a trope running through stage tragedy and moral tales. But in the case of wards, stopping to look at the lives and exploitation of female wards opens up so much about this microcosm of exploitation, profit and abuse.

A typical example is the story of the woman who started out as a ward of Ralph Rokeby at Bishop Burton in 1524, a place rented from Cardinal Wolsey. She was Anne Cresacre, and her destiny eventually was to marry the son of Sir Thomas More. F.W. Brooks, writing in the 1950s, explains how this came to be:

> Anne's father had died when she was barely a year old, and Rokeby, possibly by a corrupt bargain with a lawyer who married Anne's mother, and, it was hinted, was keeping a goodly part of Anne's inheritance for the term of her mother's life, had taken possession of Anne and

> had married her, at the age of nine … to his son, John, who was about the same age.

Anne was then forcibly abducted by Sir Robert Constable, who arrived at Rokeby with a massive force of fighting men; she was taken to the home of Brian Hastings, and then to the house owned by John Nowell, where he married Anne to his young son Thomas, who was around her age. Anne was a royal ward, and she was being passed like a chattel. But onwards she went again, later to become married into the More family, and today history records her as a family member as painted by the great painter Holbein, held in the royal collection.

Abductions became part of the pattern of Tudor life among the rich. F.W. Brooks offers an insight into the rough nature of all this, and one story does not even concern a rich man, but a servant:

> Robert Dyon, a poor serving man, being contracted in marriage with Margaret Normanton, left her in service with Sir Edward Maddison of Caister (Lincs) and went to seek his fortune promising to return and marry her soon. During his absence she was abducted by Guy Sotherby of Halton, taken across the Humber and privily married to Thomas, his son, who speedily consummated the marriage though his bride was only thirteen.

This was all about ownership of people and transactions of profit regarding alliances and possession; under coverture, there were countless ways available to command and restrict women's lives. The old Norman concept persisted, and the Tudors made most of the possibilities of exploiting any area of economic success and control.

Once again, the genius of Shakespeare reveals many layers of potential change and radical thought around women's various helplessness in the forms of slavery and suppression to which they were subject. Running through his plays we have the strong women, women in power, from Cleopatra to Portia, and it is in the words of Lady Macbeth that he gives what must have been a shocking portrait of a mind capable of murder, when she says 'Thou art too full of the milk of human kindness/to catch the nearest way' when her husband waivers at the thought of taking a life. If we contrast this with these lines from *The Taming of the Shrew*, it can be seen what was the norm for a wife, and how far from this is Lady Macbeth:

> Such duty as the subject owes the prince,
> Even such a woman oweth to her husband.

Chapter 7

Recusant Suffering and Extreme Exits

In October 1540, Henry VIII went to Hull to inspect the battlements and defences of the town. He saw that there were weaknesses on the Humber estuary side, and ordered a castle and blockhouses to be built, and he wanted them 'mighty strong'. Today, driving eastwards towards Hedon and Spurn, the traveller sees no remnants of what was, in the sixteenth century, a great and sturdy ace of clubs-shaped fortification, comprised of a castellar entrance, a courtyard and dungeons. The latter, known as the 'blockhouses', were to be the gaols of the Catholic recusants of Yorkshire in the opposition known as the Pilgrimage of Grace.

This planning was done in the aftermath of the dissolution of the monasteries, and so there was plenty of local stone available for the building work. At the time there were the institutions of Blackfriars, Whitefriars and a Carthusian priory around the area. Joseph Hirst, writing in 1913, noted the profits Henry made here: 'The cash received by Henry VIII, as the result of the dissolution of the monasteries, is shown to be between fourteen and fifteen million pounds sterling in present money value.'

After the revolt, there were the actions of revenge already recounted, and a sketch in the British Museum shows the location of the triple gallows where John Hallam, Thomas Walters and John Proude, Hull principals in the Pilgrimage of Grace, were hanged. Local feeling against Henry was no doubt critical and vicious against the king, as not only these leaders, but also Sir Robert Constable (whom we met in the previous chapter) was hanged in chains, as a contemporary letter of 1537 describes: 'On Friday, being market day at Hull, Sir Robert Constable suffered, and doth hang in chains, as this bearer can show you, and I think his bones will hang there these hundred years.'

The Tudor chronicler Raphael Holinshed describes the wording of the law when a sentence of being hanged alive in chains was applied:

> But if he be convicted of wilful murther, done either upon pretended malice or in any noble robbery, he is either hanged alive in chains near the place where the fact was committed or else, upon compassion being taken, first strangled with a rope, and so continued till his bones consume to nothing. And where wilful manslaughter is perpetrated, the offender hath his right hand first stricken off.

The hanging in chains procedure was the established doom for the crime of piracy, and Execution Dock in London was the scene of many such agonising exits from the world. The conclusion in the case of Constable has to be that he was seen as a particularly dangerous and worrying rebel leader.

The 'Popish recusants' were so called after the lawmaking in the wake of the Act of Uniformity of 1534. They were labelled Popish Recusants Convict. At this point there has to be some explanation of the Acts against recusants that became known as the Penal Laws, and these began in 1558 with the first passing of a penal statute. The Acts that followed up to the early years of the reign of Elizabeth were the laws that employed four iron stanchels, with hooks, for the hanging of the unacceptable religious practice. There were stages of punishment for each offence, so that for instance ministers had to use the Book of Common Prayer. Penalty for not doing this:

> First offence – six months in gaol and a fine of a year's income.

> Second offence – deprivation of office and a year in gaol.
> Third offence – imprisonment for life.

In 1562 the Act was all about the printed word and religious teaching. It also issued the death penalty for people who took issue with the supremacy of the monarch, if they did this twice. The main legislation through the years between *c.*1560 and 1584 dealt with the administration of the mass, movement of foreign priests, and the education of priests.

Under Elizabeth then, the Hull blockhouses became busy, full of people who kept to the beliefs and practices of their faith. The prisoners were rooted out of homes and hiding places by *poursuivants*, and Joseph Hirst, writing of the blockhouses, recorded: 'In Christmas Eve, 1594 at midnight … another poursuivant, was sent to search a house in or about Winsley Wood, and there he met Anthony Atkinson, the searcher of Hull, who had brought with him thirty men. They entered the place, and after breaking down the walls, arrested Mr. Warcop, Sadler, two menservants and Father Anthony Rawlings, who were all afterwards imprisoned.'

Elizabeth employed hundreds of priest hunters, and it has been claimed that for the search undertaken for a Father Haywood, 600 *poursuivants* were paid. Priests on the run hid wherever they could find warmth and shelter; they hid in woods, and were hunted out by dogs, and Joseph Hirst notes that when caught they 'were arrested, hanged, drawn, bowelled and quartered'. If the reader has ever wondered what costs were involved in such executions, there is this listing from Newcastle:

> Paid to a Frenchman which did take forth the seminary priest's bowels after hanging 20s
>
> For coals, which made the fire of the seminary priest 6d
>
> For a hand axe and a cutting knife which did rip and quarter the seminary priest 14d

> For a horse which trailed him from the sledge to the gallows 12d
>
> For four iron stanchels with hooks, for the hanging of the seminary's four Quarters on the four gates 3s 8d
>
> To a mason for two days' work, setting the stanchels of the gates fast 20d

The stories of the inmates of the blockhouses may surely only be partially imagined; one may assume high levels of torture and deprivation, and a disregard for human life or for any principles of thought and intellect that the recusants had. The horrendous list from Newcastle shows exactly how the prisoners were defined and handled: as considerately as tripe in an abattoir. There are many biographies, but perhaps this summary of the experience of Edmund Sykes of Leeds from 1585 is representative. He had been imprisoned once, and then went to Europe. After that, this was the rest of his life:

> He quickly returned to England, and after some time was taken again. Of his second imprisonment it is recorded by Dr. Champney in the manuscript annals … preserved at Douai, that after some years fruitfully employed in the vineyards of the Lord, being apprehended, was thrust into a most strait and very troublesome prison, in which, by the experience of suffering, he acquired the virtue of patience and learned to die. Afterwards. Being brought to the bar, and arraigned for high treason, for being made a priest … he was sentenced to die, according to which he was hanged, bowelled and quartered on the 23 rd March, 1587.
>
> His prison sufferings extended from August 1585 to that date.

There were women prisoners in the blockhouses, and we see some references in the records, such as Alicia Dauson and Joanna Hugh in 1600. The latter was described as *diaconum* (deaconess). Janet Adams died in a blockhouse in 1590 and 'Bernard and wife were delivered upon bond' to go back into their daily lives, but this seems not to be the pleasant fate of 'Milburn and his wife'. Then, in among the forgotten names, we have on record the name of Anne Teshe, the name of a close friend of Margaret Clitherow, and one of a group of women – 'twenty of fifty three … dragged to hear sermons' in 1600, and this leads to arguably the most celebrated recusant in Elizabeth's reign. This is Margaret Clitherow of York.

Margaret was a goodwife of a butcher in York's now heritage-rich street of The Shambles, and visitors may walk by her home and shrine, as she is now Saint Margaret and she escaped the blockhouse or the York prison for one repulsive reason: she was pressed to death. This punishment was for those accused who would not plead. It was known as a death of *peine forte et dure* (tough and hard) and involved the offender being laid flat and weighed down by a succession of heavy stones across a plank of wood, so that death was gradual and agonising. There was much more to this than mere application of weights. As the aficionado of torture, Geoffrey Abbott explains: '… he should have no sustenance, save only on the first day three morsels of bread, and on the second day three draughts of water that should be nearest to the prison door and that should be his daily ration till he died … or till he answered'.

What had Margaret Clitherow done to deserve this? She had kept to her faith and beliefs. She was born in 1556, and her father was a chandler and was at one time sheriff of the city of York. Under the recusant troubles she began to be noticed doing unpopular things, such as visiting prisoners, and even worse, she gave cover to visiting priests from Europe and was fined. For a while, her influential husband covered her misdeeds and she survived, but her actions led to a spell in York Castle in 1583. However, on her freedom, there she was with a secret mass location and this was eventually revealed. She was tried in early 1586. It would have come as a shock to the judges to hear her say that in her opinion she was not guilty of an offence. This meant that she would not submit to trial by a jury.

Margaret's ill treatment and suffering was at the toll house, a place that tourists now pass as they walk from York railway station towards the shopping centre. Her death took fifteen minutes, and after her remains were buried in the dung, her body was later reclaimed and taken for a burial in which there was dignity and respect. Today, thousands stop by her Shambles house and learn about her very remarkable life and death.

Throughout the Tudor years, there was a succession of legislation that led to long suffering and brutal exits from this world, and the recusant deaths under Elizabeth and the Protestant deaths under Mary were merely two areas that are now well known, through heritage and popular culture. The fact is that underlying the legislation was the common practice of applying horrendous and inhumane sentences. There were still local and regional instances of tough and barbarous judicial killings, and one much-reported example is that of the Halifax gibbet. There was a Gibbet Law in operation, and this was explained by a writer called Bentley in 1761, when he wrote, '… if a felon be taken within the liberty or precincts of the said forest [Hardwick] and taken [cloth] or any other commodity of the value of thirteen pence one ha'penny that they shall after three markets within the town of Halifax … shall be taken to the gibbet and there have his head cut off from his body.' Between 1541 and 1650 the public records show fifty-three beheaded.

The ancient gibbet rulings stretch back to the days of an urgent need of protection for those travellers who were moving around with their cloth, subject to robbers at any time. The legal representative here was the High Bailiff, working under the liberty – a crown franchise in effect – and acting as both executioner and administrator. The gibbet itself was, in the words of a Victorian historian, '… an axe attached to a square block of wood, four and a half feet long … drawn up between two upright posts by a cord and pulley, and fastened to a pin … At a given signal, the pin was pulled out, the axe fell, and the head of the culprit was severed from the body.' During Elizabeth's reign, victims of the gibbet included Nicholas Hewett de North and Thomas Malone in May 1587, and it comes as no surprise to learn that they were logged as 'vagrants'. Several women were also beheaded, and their names were recorded using the Latin for 'wife', which is *uxor*. A typical entry is that of 'Ux. Samuel Etall, on account of many thefts. Beheaded Aug. 28, 1630'.

A survey of repulsive judicial killings under the Tudors would not be complete without considering a specific piece of death penalty legislation passed in 1531 that, as Geoffrey Abbott points out, 'included the name of the individual against whom the punishment was to be levied, instead of being couched in more general terms'. Looking at his offence, a mass poisoning at the home of the Bishop of Rochester, one wonders if there was not some personal vengeance involved. The cook, Richard Rouse, was the man convicted. The special Act of Parliament has these words about Rouse's crime: 'porridge or gruel was forthwith made … whereby not only the number seventeen persons of the said family … were mortally infected or poisoned, and one of them, Bennet Curwan, gentleman, is thereof deceased … Alice Trypitt, widow, is also thereof now deceased.'

The Act was repealed in 1547, but during the short time of its life, the bill brought about the deaths of three people. Geoffrey Abbott, always a writer to enjoy the gruesome sides of criminal history, reminds his readers that in France, boiling alive thrived for a while, and he gives an account of such a death (and that of the executioner also) in 1488 which includes these words: 'The executioner … tried two or three times to sink the malefactor with a great iron hook and forthwith several persons … approached the executioner as he lay with his face on the ground and gave him so many blows that he died here he lay.'

There were also the executions that were clearly meant to be significant and fearful for the masses of common people who were living at the time already discussed, regarding what might be called adventurous thinking. That is to say, deaths to discourage flamboyant and radical lines of thought and unacceptable action. The Holy Maid of Kent case, as has been seen, was a typical example. With examples such as the boiling alive legislation, what emerges throughout the late sixteenth century is a stress on excessively violent and barbarous deaths within the criminal justice systems. Such manners of execution and prolonged torture had been common across Europe for centuries.

Andrew McCall, in his work on crime through the medieval centuries, *The Medieval Underworld*, provides ample cases of such things as amputation, boiling alive, branding, burning, garrotting and embowelling. Our general images of punishment in the story of the Tower of London generally include the use of the rack and the wheel, as well as pressing and branding. McCall describes the gradual transition from the earlier law codes pre the Plantagenets, and sums up the problems in this way: 'In the general turmoil of the early Middle Ages, it was no easy task for either the church or its new allies, the Christian kings, to prevent the independent-spirited warrior from taking the law into his own hands and visiting his own justice on his enemies.'

Up to Henry VIII's church and state reformation, one needs to recall that the local church power was over life and death. An outstanding example of this is in a story from York, where there was a prison held by the Archbishop, and this may be seen on prints and drawings before 1829, when the Minster was burnt by Jonathan Martin and the prison may be seen nestling in the frame of the building. The gallows in place names across England often indicate local church or manorial gallows, and this provides yet more evidence that sees the relevant line of thought about the nature of Tudor justice being often too far from centres of control such as the regional councils like the one in York or the Welsh Marches to have a real knowledge of crime in the boondocks.

Looking at the medieval period through modern eyes, it is hard to imagine the complex structures of the authority of both crown and church in all areas of an individual's life and death in that Catholic universe. The higher clergy had a high level of personal status and sway among their flock, and the wealth of the church went along with this. Of course, they had their own courts as well, and their provinces were centres of great influence.

The old Ainsty area of York was integral to the Benedictine Priory at Micklegate, and the priory of Holy Trinity was a powerful establishment, with rights given to it by the king reaching back to Henry I. One of those rights was the power over criminals who were apprehended within the Ainsty; this meant that such persons could be hanged in the area, and there was a priory scaffold. King Stephen had granted land to the priory, and as the gallows stood there, it was known for some time as 'the thieves' gallows'. A chronicle of hangings in the city begins with what is arguably the strangest of all the tales, because in fact the accused in question survived the hanging.

The man in question was John Ellenstreng. All we know about his offence is that he was 'convicted of larcenies' and so sentenced to hang; he was a member of the Guild of the Hospital of St John of Jerusalem, and luckily for him, his fellow monks were allowed to take away the bodies of any of their number who had dangled from the scaffold. They came for him to give him a Christian burial, and when they arrived at their chapel (St James on the Mount) to their amazement, John was still breathing. As was usually the case in the medieval centuries, myths were generated from this maintaining that he had been saved by blessed intervention – that St James himself had saved John's life.

The man who had been 'hanged' on 18 August was given a pardon later by the king himself, after there had been a written account of the strange event by a witness, a man called John de Vallibus, who was one of the justices in the Eyre (circuit court) of York.

This local power, and the presence of church authority in justice, was of course, changed after 1536, but execution and extreme punishment still had a place in Tudor arrangements for hangings and other methods of removal of felons. Andrew McCall sums up the situation before the arrival of the Tudors: 'The King or the Emperor, by virtue of his theoretical position at the apex of the feudal pyramid, remained the fountain of secular justice, the guardian of order and law …' This was materially the same as Henry VIII had made the scenario in the mid-1530s.

Bringing reflections on all these woeful tales of horrendous executions at the hands of the courts, there is often a tendency to forget that there were other reasons, on top of sheer desire to provide retribution. After all, the destiny of the fallen soul was hell or perhaps purgatory. The state had to provide barbarous killings because this would supposedly send a signal to all other potential wrongdoers; it also had to create visible, tortuous suffering in a Mosaic Law stance of vengeance. The assumption was simple: the felon took a life by applying pain and terror, and so now the law of our country will do exactly the same. This was an age without mass media. The whole process of murder investigation and trial was ritualistic as well as practical.

On the advent of a suspicious death, the coroner would usually have the corpse laid on a table in a tavern, so that people could look on and identify the body, so that identity was certain, as far as could be established. Then basic information would be gathered and assessed, and usually the verdict of the coroner's court in such cases was wilful murder by person or persons unknown. The necessity of further investigation would be undertaken by the magistrate, the sheriff and any *poursuivants* brought in to take their part, as we have seen in the recusant narratives. From the medieval years, the coroner (previously the crowner) would be the principal officer of law in the case.

As Shani D'Cruze and others have stated, 'the collective psychic response [to murder] has strong emotional dimensions to it. Murder, because of its appalling nature, evokes feelings in us all, but especially for the immediate victims of the event …' The magistrates and lawmakers of the Tudors may not have had that criminological vocabulary, but they knew that contextual point about the impact of the offence. In later years, when there was more ritual at Tyburn hangings, a 'last dying speech' was expected. In a work of 1829 on trials at York, the author, Leman Rede, took several pages at the close of each murder trial story to reflect on the Christian implications and references of a confession and a passionate, open confession of wrongdoing.

While the media today pay endless attention to the death of Anne Boleyn in May 1536, and the mystery of the princes in the Tower, the focus of crime history needs to give a place to the ordinary people who died heroically at the Tyburn in Newgate, such as Anne Askew, a friend of Catherine Parr, Henry VIII's last wife of the famous six. She was yet another victim of the elastic crime of heresy, for allegedly working on the mind of the queen to convert her. She is in the records, one might argue, as most horrendously subject to the torments of the rack, applied to her in the White Tower. The records show that she 'quietly and patiently' was 'praying to the Lord ... she endured their tyranny till her bones and joints were almost plucked asunder'. She died at the stake in Smithfield.

It was at Newgate that one finds the notorious 'Tyburn Tree' and the first hangings there were logged in June 1571. Newgate is first noted as a place of punishment in 1218, and the first record of any check on the place in terms of supervision is in 1334, when, in the words of a Victorian journal, '... an inquiry was made into the condition of the unfortunate inmates, and many of the atrocities practised were brought to light'. The same record describes the conditions, and explains that in 1422, Richard Whittington, the famous Lord Mayor, 'left a large sum of money for the rebuilding of Newgate, in the course of which the cells were not only made more habitable, but an extension of the prison by running two wings down Newgate Street ...'

The Triple Tree, so named for its three facilities for hanging victims, suggests the nature of the execution of felons was industrial, to say the least. When fully charged with the condemned, the tree could deal with twenty-four people; the signs are clear that, as was to be the case until public hangings were abolished in 1868, Tyburn deaths were merely one of many public attractions at the fair, and the first victim in this ghastly place was a celebrity, Robert Story, a man who was accused of, in the words of the Treason Act of 1351, 'encompassing the death of the sovereign'. In this case, the sovereign was Elizabeth, and particularly as Story had also been charged with espionage she was allowed no space for thoughts of mercy to creep in.

Story was born in 1504, and he had absconded into the Netherlands when the hunt was on for recusants. By underhand means, he was brought back to England, and this intelligent, educated man, who had studied in Oxford and actually become a Professor of Law there, and also worked in the law, had been too reckless of expressing his opinions in public, notoriously stating: 'Woe unto thee, O land, when they king is a child …' But he had been actively involved in politics, and it took some time before he was brought to trial. His death was the standard for treason – being hanged, drawn and quartered.

The Tudor years are remembered as the decades of violent and cruel exits, and the literature supporting this image is crowned by the classic work of desperate death, Foxe's *Book of Martyrs*, published in 1563. The Rev. John Foxe was a prebend of Salisbury Cathedral, and had a living at Shipton close by. The book was a catalogue of torment and suffering, and was a phenomenal success. It is certain that the book had an impact not only on perceptions of the monarchy and the law, but, as S.T. Bindoff has commented: 'For the burnings did more than anything else to generate that "unthinking, ferocious and almost indelible" hatred which generations of otherwise tolerant and short-memoried Englishmen were to nourish towards Rome. Not for nothing was Foxe's *Book of Martyrs* to become the most widely read and possessed of English classics …'

A survey of the judicial killings and execrable tortures that went on in the blockhouses, the Tower, Newgate, York Castle and a thousand other foul locations, reveals a constant repetition of trials undertaken without due process, a rushed and immoral despatch of felons, and a disregard for the underlying principles in common law. The words of Magna Carta were erased in the midst of such inhumane practices, and those with power and authority acted with any one of a range of actions, going from whimsical to vengeful. At the very top, after 1534 was a monarch who had the powers of church and state, combined with a structure of court and law courts, royal proclamations, edicts and moody attitudes of repression.

This summary of the Tudor culture of people awash with statutes and fear of any of the many arms of justice, further reinforces the kingdom as a dangerous place to be, and a location of fearful paranoia, when we consider evidence such as Ruth Goodman's survey of the Tudors 'behaving badly' in a social nexus of image, right thinking, reputation and obedience to every stream of authority in the great ocean of law that threatened to drown individuals in apprehension and foreboding. Mistress Overdone's words in *Measure for Measure* become relevant once more:

> O, thus, what with the war, what with the sweat, what with the gallows,
>
> And what with poverty, I am custom-shrunk.

Reaching the stage of Tudor government and statecraft as it was under Elizabeth, the structures of justice have the character of a transient show set up at every stage of a circuit; if there was a new offence, a statute appeared, and there was an accused standing by or a potential case to be reviewed and possibly be the subject of scrutiny. Wrongdoers in the higher echelons could escape legal notice and trial, and examples of such cases are enlightening in a number of ways. A useful example of this is the life and atrocities of Walter Hungerford, the 1st Baron Hungerford of Heytesbury (1503–40). He was eventually charged with harbouring a priest, and was obviously a thorn in the flesh for the powers that be in spite of starting out in life as a squire to the body of Henry VIII, which was a post that made him potentially very influential in court circles.

A similar kind of insight into circles of power and influence emerge when one looks at bodies such as the Council of the North, which had immense power in Yorkshire and beyond. Here, the names are familiar, they are part of a local network, and when the nature of the bench of justices is considered, the reach and strength of their influence is always evident in local records. Even as late as the mid-1800s, it was recognised by lawyers and administrators linked to the running of the assize courts that a Welsh jury would not be inclined to convict in a Carmarthen trial, as I discovered when researching my book, *The Girl Who Lived on Air* (a case from 1869). It was in order to prevent or reduce this local network of power-brokers that the Council of the North was composed of men who had no regional allegiance.

Once the English Reformation was in full swing, the social divisions appeared at every level; power in the workings of the law too often had the scent of tight influence about it. Looked at from the twenty-first century it comes across as a law machine that was allowing some opportunity for women to be given slightly more voice in the courts, but the solid domestic and family status quo kept so many strands of local control as the male hierarchy wanted them to be. With hindsight, we may see and understand exactly what was brewing in all the hierarchical social relationships, as well as between parliament and royal power.

Chapter 8

Elizabeth in Peril

Plots, true and false, are necessary things/to raise up commonwealths, and ruin kings.

John Dryden

In 1587, James VI of Scotland wrote to Queen Elizabeth after the execution of his mother, Mary, Queen of Scots, after Elizabeth had signed the death warrant. It was the years of torment and fear for the English queen, because her cousin Mary Stuart had a strong claim to the English throne, had many allies, and had been very much an ally of the forces and regimes in Europe who were keen to see Elizabeth gone, and a Catholic monarch back on the throne. James wrote a prose larded with diplomatic agreement, summed up in the words: 'I dare not wrong you so far as not to judge honourably of your unspotted part therein …'

Elizabeth must have constantly had an eye on Scotland ever since Mary married Lord Darnley and then experienced his murder, followed by the trial of his killer, Bothwell, and his subsequent acquittal. Murder was indeed, as Shakespeare said in *Macbeth*, 'the nearest way' to achieve one's goals. For Bothwell, it had failed, in spite of his removing David Rizzio, Mary's close servant. When Mary had been confronted by three deaths – her mother, her husband and Henry II of France, she was standing alone, and trusted in a future in England; coming south, instead of any kind of welcome, she faced prison, and was incarcerated in a number of gaols. A prisoner's life was her future: there she was, a queen, in endless house arrest, but able to write letters. We now know, thanks to the brilliant work of scholars and codebreakers Tomokiyo, Bierman, Lasry and Courtney, that she wrote hundreds of letters in code, managing to have them smuggled out and even placed in ambassadorial communications. We also know that there was a 'mole' and that the spymaster Robert Walsingham knew about her activities.

Revolt was in the air for years. She and her cousin were at the heart of a maelstrom of dynastic rivalry, relying on supposed friends and on illicit methods of being informed and issuing requests. She summed up in one letter: 'Watch out for Walsingham. He's a clever man and a deceiver.' But the fears from Scotland and Mary's status were real enough. She was the grand daughter of Margaret, Henry VIII's sister, and daughter of James V of Scotland. Other rivals to Elizabeth had been removed, but Mary remained.

Mary was in Sheffield State Prison for some time, and a Victorian historian describes this:

> One wintry morning, near the end of the year 1570, the accomplished and unfortunate Mary Queen of Scots was brought across the hills from Chatsworth in the custody of the Earl of Shrewsbury and his men to his castle at Sheffield, as a remote and strong seclusion, capable of resisting any possible attack, and where she might lie hid in lonely durance until forgotten by her scheming friends …

However, as she was shut up in Yorkshire, plots were afoot to the north and in Europe. The Catholic missionary priests, described earlier in the tales of the recusants, were intriguing with supportive Catholic gentlemen and with aristocrats across various countries. One result of this was a war of words and propaganda in sermons, tracts and correspondence. One of the martyrs, Edmund Campion, put forward arguments defending the subversive thinking of himself and his fellow protesters, because of course they were being defined as traitors and condemned to death. He reasoned that when the Protestants condemned the priests they were acting against their own ancestors, and that England had always been 'the island of saints, and the most devoted child of the See of Peter'.

The hot issue of exactly what crimes were being committed by those priests and scholars became universal. As historian Alison Plowden put it: 'Campion's death provoked a barrage of pamphlets which kept the printers working overtime on both side of the Channel.' There was such a stir that the English had to make some kind of statement, and the result was most likely the work of Thomas Norton – *A Declaration of Favourable Dealing by Her Majesty's Commissioners for the Examination of Certain Traitors.* It is known today that torture was applied to offenders guilty of serious crime, so it may be seen what was going on – a cover-up, a faux scholarly defence of extreme methods. Again, Alison Plowden explains exactly how these species of traitors were seen at home: 'The missionaries were Englishmen born who had chosen to transfer their allegiance to the Queen's avowed enemies.'

What had to be propounded across the land was that the prosecutions of the priests were not related to religious beliefs. The obvious path to take on the offensive was to keep firmly, in the persecutions, to the words of the fourteenth-century treason legislation. Consequently, knowing that Catholic opinion of the current queen was that she was illegitimate, heretic, and moreover, someone who had been excommunicated by the Holy Father, defining treason was a much simple affair that swapping opinions on the practice and dogma in varieties of Christian belief, and soon there was concern that various factions were 'encompassing the death' of the sovereign. Treason could be investigated by means of torture. The rack would be used, and other horrendous methods of extracting information and confessions.

In 1583 it had become apparent that there were to be attempts on Elizabeth's life. A coup d'état was planned. Conferences of conspirators were held, and there was a plan of invasion. Locations for landing troops, army numbers and scale of attack, and identities of leaders were topics discussed. Matters were being intensified. Information then spread. In a letter to the Cardinal of Como, the nuncio of the Pope wrote: 'The Duke of Guise and the Duke of Mayenne have told me that they have a plot for killing the Queen of England by the hand of a Catholic, though not one outwardly, who is near her person and is ill-affected towards her for having put to death one of his Catholic relations.'

In 1584 events occurred that spurred on extreme reactions in the ranks of Elizabeth's top advisers such as Robert Cecil and Walsingham himself, the chief spymaster. In July of that year William of Orange (Protestant) was shot and killed as he walked up the stairs in his house. Even worse for the government, there had been a design from a young man called Somerville to kill the queen. He appears to have been a lone fanatic, who vowed to kill her and 'set her head on a pole'. The consequences of these things were inevitably extreme. A declaration of a concept above the law was made, and it was called The Bond. Alison Plowden defines this:

> The bond which this association were to sign went through several drafts, but in its final form – the form in which it was circulated throughout the towns and shires that autumn and winter – it was a straight invitation to lynch law. The signatories, tens of thousands of them, bound themselves by a solemn oath …

The oath was to react to offenders towards the queen in this way: 'to prosecute such persons unto death and to act the utmost revenge upon them'. Where was the rule of law, we have to ask? Where were the English values as in the common law? The situation was seen as a state of war. The Bond suggests both a growing paranoia and a strong will to meet any violent action with a more violent one. When some material was found belonging to a Father Creighton, there were words describing anarchy and ruin across the whole Tudor realm. Such was the panic involved that a statute issued was the Act for the Queen's Safety. Such pressures came along with fears of revolt and insurrection that there was a faction working to make The Bond association into law, and against there were voices speaking out for moderation. Yet, whatever the outcome there had to be strong and decisive action taken.

In the mist of all this apprehension and fears about invasion and assassination there came the Throckmorton Plot of 1583. Sir Francis Throckmorton was arrested in 1583 and languished in the Tower until the following July. He was a member of a well-known Catholic family, and had been influenced while travelling in Europe by some Catholic figures involved in open dissent. Such was Francis's involvement that he came home to accept a role as a messenger for Mary. This is the point at which those shady figures, the ambassadors, begin to bc much more than mere diplomats with charm and good manners. The French ambassador, Michel de Castelnau, was involved, and it comes as no surprise to find that one of Walsingham's men, known as Fagot, revealed what was happening. Throckmorton was involved closely, as becomes obvious from the fact that he was actually working on a cipher when he was found and arrested. A French diplomat, Mendoza, was also known to be involved, and surely he was fortunate to be merely expelled rather than placed in a Tower cell.

Throckmorton was surely a very active advocate for assassination, with feelers reaching out to other circles of treasonable nature, and he influenced a further plot, the Babington planned killing a few years later. Babington had been a page with Mary Stuart, and he intended to kill Elizabeth and support Mary in power. Another agent from Walsingham had him arrested in executed in 1586. As for Throckmorton: here we face the issue of the use of torture. The case made the conspirator quite a celebrity. There was an anonymous ballad on his execution called *The Lamentation of Englande* (1584), which said what many such popular verses did: show the criminal to be lacking in moral fibre as well as a right-thinking intellect by referring to his 'shameful end'. But God was at work for England, the poet stresses:

> Even so the Lord by his great might,
> my comfort doth maintain,
> in keeping and preserving still,
> my Prince from traitors traine,
> and did preserve her from the harmes
> Throckmorton did pretende:
> who even at Tyborne for the same,
> did make a shameful ende. Pray, pray etc.
>
> (*Prince*: a word referring to any ruler, therefore, to Elizabeth)

Throckmorton's doom was the dreaded rack. In the Tower of London, this was one of several torture devices, including the thumbscrew, the Cave of Roses and the water drop torment. The rack itself was introduced into the Tower equipment in the reign of Henry VI in the time of the Constable, John Holland. It was in the shape of a horse trough, into which the prisoner was placed. Two windlasses were positioned at either end, and as they were pulled, the force dislocating the person's shoulders and other joints. The windlasses were extremely strong. Sir George Younghusband, writing almost a century ago, explains, 'So powerful were these windlasses that sufficient pressure could be brought to dislocate the shoulders and even the knee joints and hips. The refinement in this class of torture lay in the advantage whilst it did not kill the victim … it caused the most excruciating suffering.'

Geoffrey Abbott, quoted earlier, was a writer with a dark interest in torture, and he pointed out in his reference work on horrendous torture devices that although the Romans were the first to invest a rack torture, England was superior in the art of inflicting pain. He explains: 'The English model was infinitely more painful than that of the Romans, because the victim was at floor level and would have to be hoisted to the level of the rack frame by ropes, the victim's own body weight exacerbating the agony as he was slowly raised, every inch threatening to dislocate his joints.' Almost beyond belief is the recorded habit of whipping the prisoner as he was being stretched, but this did happen in Germany.

The Tower had its fair share of suffering traitors who had schemed to either kill the queen or to stage a coup. The events of the 1580s, culminating of course in the attempt by Spain to send the Armada to land an army on English shores, was one of extreme national fear and threats to the peace of the land, in addition to the dangers to monarch and government, and every 5 November we are reminded of the Gunpowder Plot of 1605, which followed on from these earlier plots and plans to restore a Catholic sovereign. At the core of this sense of insecurity was also the inescapable anxiety over the hard fact that Elizabeth had no successor. Back in the 1570s it had seemed to many that she would marry the Earl of Leicester, Robert Dudley, but he was to wed Lettice Knollys in secret, and had to wait to be forgiven.

It is now known, after research by Tracy Borman involving study of the revised edition of William Camden's *Annals of Queen Elizabeth* in 1615 when James I was conceiving of an edited view of recent history, his directions to Camden show a text that has changed our view of this succession. James instructed the historian to cover and reconstruct his earlier statement about the queen's last words regarding the inheritor of the throne. This shows that she made no instruction that 'the Scottish king' should succeed. Of course, James wanted that put right.

This research shows once again what a fractious, fragile and nervous time these years between the mid-1580s to the succession were, packed with plots, invasions, planned rebellions and head-to-head confrontations in intellectual debate between speakers and writers of different faiths. Elizabeth was assailed on all sides, from the Scottish threat to the French and Papal opposition, and from the machinations of diplomats and Mary's coded letters.

The result of all this was that the workings of criminal law were given a very sharp edge, and this cut beyond moral restraints and feeble arguments. It was an age of suspicion when one's words were chosen carefully, and also an age of sensitivity, when international relations were seeped in hidden design. In the midst of this, law became flexible, and subject to individual strength and power.

If one needed to seek out a confirmation of this tendency of law to fail before individuals, the case of Bothwell and his murder of Darnley is a perfect example. Magnus Magnusson summarises the 'trial' of the killer very strongly:

> As a Privy Councillor, Bothwell was one of those who arranged the proceedings. He had been packing the city with four thousand of his tough Border adherents for days. Lennox, who was permitted by law to bring only six supporters, marched from Glasgow with a body of three thousand men, but turned back when he was challenged at Linlithgow by Bothwell's men. As a result there was no accuser in court.

Sometimes a system of criminal law tends to fall down very easily in the face of attitudes dominated by pragmatism; in Elizabeth's time, that pragmatism was led by the fist more often than the diplomatic chat.

Niccolo Machiavelli would have been very pleased.

Chapter 9

Coasting and Corsairs

Piracy – like smuggling – was altogether too lucrative and half the countryside was in league with the offenders.

H. Alker Tripp

A survey of reference works on the sixteenth century reveals a curious aspect of crime history: the absence of much material on the organised crimes of smuggling and piracy. This is a trend in true crime summaries generally, and it is not easy to see why. In J.A. Sharpe's volume, dealing with crime in society between 1550 and 1750, there is no mention of piracy, and although his observation that '… eighteen century observers estimated that 3,000,000lbs of tea were smuggled into the country annually', he does not venture backwards to see origins and sources of this fact.

Earlier reference works covering crime in general over the centuries usually select well-known figures from the annals of piracy such as Sir Francis Drake, and often point out the fact, in the words of Sir Harold Scott, 'privateering was, in fact, legalised piracy' and he does give an overall explanation of the law in this respect: 'In the reign of Elizabeth I, English and Welsh pirates were severely punished in home waters, but tolerated and even encouraged if they preyed on Spanish shipping lanes.'

Other tomes with the intention of surveying crime across a whole culture often have no entry at all under 'Piracy'. Over the years, in the historiography of writing on real crime, the commercial imperative has given 'bloody murder' and other crimes of violence precedence over offences labelled 'social crime' such as poaching and smuggling. For piracy and smuggling, there has always been their slot in mass media narratives reserved for derivative images from *Treasure Island* and then later Hollywood film productions. The result has been a set of stereotypes and a number of fixed ideas about who pirates were and what they did. As far as the tourists trails are concerned, there is Execution Dock and tales of pirate corpses dangling in the sea breeze down the Thames. This goes back to the stories in *The Newgate Calendar* (discussed in the next chapter) such as that of 'Captain John Kidd, who suffered for piracy at Execution Dock, May 22, 1701' and his character profile has these words: 'In a word, his ruling passion appeared to be avarice; and to this was owing his connection with the pirates.'

The legislation against piracy is rooted in a statute of Henry VIII. This was the Offences at Sea Act of 1536, and, as usual, it designated the offence as capital for 'all treasons, felonies, robberies, murthers and confederacies committed in or upon the sea'. The wording covers everything, but naturally, when there was so much war around Europe involving frequent travel by sea (as in Spain and the Netherlands for instance), some kind of application was needed to allow a government to use any maritime resource. Hence along came the corsairs, the privateers, and it has to be said that this was just another form of piracy with another name. This is because the concept of a letter of marque, sometimes called a letter of reprisal, proved to be a useful cover for nefarious practice. If one nation was at war with another, a privateer could be used, with such a letter, to board and take a vessel as if the action was defined as an approach to a force in opposition. Consequently, long before the Tudors, the practice established was that a privateer could be on the watch for a vessel that could be exploited, and the act would be legally sanctioned.

These licences were first issued around 1240, and the first such letter on record issued in England was in 1295. This most questionable enterprise was in effect a green light for a ship owner to invent a 'reprisal' of some kind, so that he could apply to the Court of Admiralty for his licence to act in a reprisal. The letter of reprisal was in this way a disguise, a sham, in practice, and waving the letter could become carte blanche for piracy. In effect, the letters were privateering commissions hiding under a sham of a response to offence.

The truth was that, in a nation with very little sea power at that time, the kinds of piracy operated by privateers was a useful tool for the authorities. In practice it meant that a privateer with a licence could use a letter of marque, and so piracy moved around in disguise, as it were, in a society which, when it came to the hard facts of life, depended on such activities for trade and survival. In the context of piracy well away from home, other liberties were used, in quasi-governmental enterprises.

A standard example of this would be Drake's flotilla that set out across the Atlantic on his major voyage, which involved rounding the Horn; Drake had absolute power, and law was effected on the spot. When he saw a mutiny stirring, his remedy was to 'try' the leading insurgent and apply the ultimate punishment, and so rule by fear.

The wider policy from the later sixteenth century was to require the local authorities and businesses to provide their own security and escorts for merchantmen, as piracy began to be a more serious problem in the waters around Britain. Large pirate outfits could operate north into Scotland, south to the coast of France and Spain, and even further away. Therefore strategies to combat piracy in any comprehensive way were formidably expensive and presented tough logistical problems.

Looking at the summaries of material in the State Papers once again opens up some curtailed narratives that nonetheless tell stories about pirate presence in specific places, and about possible degrees of success in hunting them down, sometimes, at least. This is an example from 1576–77 with South Wales as the context:

> Dec. 6: Newport. Justice of the Peace to repair immediately to Newport for the apprehension of a ship taken by John Callis the pirate, now at Newport.
>
> Jan. 12: Instructions for the better direction of such as shall have licence to pass the seas for the taking of pirates and sea rovers, to be annexed to their commissions.
>
> Note by the judge of the Admiralty for the sending of some persons as are accused of giving assistance to Callis and other pirates in Wales.
>
> Jan. 21: The Council of the ruling of the marches of Wales: Direct that the case of David Wiottye, a pirate, and others of like nature, be referred to the Court of Admiralty.

It seems not too much of an assumption to see that actions were taken against Callis, and that he was being pursued. Also of interest is the definite article in the first entry: 'John Callis the pirate'. Clearly, he was known and had been noted before this date.

As was noted in a feature provided by the Guildhall Library, 'To say simply that English piracy flourished during the last part of the 16th century is a gross understatement of the situation. It had, in fact, achieved the status of a recognised profession.' This operated with the use of the letter of marque. This franking of piratical actions, so that profits could be garnered by more parties than the actual robbers, made life on the waves always likely to spark skirmishes and even full-scale wars, as these kinds of robberies were guaranteed to provoke anyone with any power. Other criminal problems would also accrue when there was too much authority located in one captain. Mutiny is a clear example here. Peter Earle, writing of the early Stuart years and post-Civil War period, explains: 'In 1669 a real mutiny did take place … the whole crew of the Edward led by the mate simply took over the ship in Chesapeake Bay, since the captain had ordered a change of course … Other crews simply refused to weigh anchor and set sail, maybe because the ship was leaking …' But Earle adds, 'No violence was offered in the above examples … But this was not always the case … Most men carried personal weapons …'

It was a dangerous game, the border between our image today of a Royal Navy ship contrasted with a privateer, only partially sanctioned. Small episodes of piracy and smuggling are often found in scores of works and records, across many genres of writing, because the literature of local history is so rich and diverse, and these hint at the bigger picture. Such is the case with the writings of H. Alker Tripp, a former police officer who began writing about Suffolk in the Edwardian years. He gives instances such as this, which show how the small world of one coastal location at times met head-to-head with central powers:

> Although Henry VII and VIII, our first kings who were really alive to the importance of maritime affairs, made great efforts towards protection and ordering of sea-borne trade, piracy was rampant in the days of Elizabeth. John Flicke, of Woodbridge, was a 'regular receiver' of pirates' booty, and was continually being fined. The traffic was perpetual. In 1579 five gentlemen of Woodbridge were ordered to appear before the Privy Council to answer an accusation that Arithway Newport, a notorious pirate, had escaped arrest through their connivance. Piracy – like smuggling – was altogether too lucrative and half the countryside was in league with the offenders.

Incidentally, this Newport was possibly none other than Christopher Newport (1561–1617), who was one of the adventurers out to the Spanish Main, and who was christened at Harwich, Essex, in Tripp's area of knowledge; he married in Harwich, and was a master mariner at first in trade with London. He commanded several vessels, and in his maritime plundering his most notable success was probably the attack on the Portuguese ship *Madre de Deus* in 1592.

One story within the Elizabethan years that typifies the nature of piracy is the life and adventures of Grace O'Malley (born *c.*1530 and died in 1603). Narratives of her range from the legendary to the mythical, and a scan of mainstream sources provide practically no mention of her. Such well-established works covering Irish history as Robert Kee's *The Green Flag* series give no reference to her. But interest has been rekindled as scholars have looked afresh at prominent women in the Tudor years, and her life has even figured on television. There is even one suggestion that her pirate fleet, working off the west of Ireland, was largely one of coracles. In fact, she would have to have had galleons with lateen sails to act as she did, moving her forces swiftly to pillage and rob.

She was born into the O'Malley clan, in an Ireland, as already indicated, which was not a nation, but a collection of regional clans with their chieftains. Her father was such a leader, and they had a steady income from charging taxes on travellers; even Philip of Spain paid the clan a sizeable fee for travel. Grace sailed with her brother and father, going beyond Ireland for their booty. By 1545 she was accompanying her father on raids into France and Spain. They were no amateur bunch of chancers; they used mercenaries, sometimes including the gallowglasses of Scotland. She started a family, marrying Donal O'Flaherty, and they had two sons. And by 1564 her father was dead and she became clan leader. Settling in Clare Island, she gathered a force of several hundred men and became a major player among the families settled beyond The Pale.

Her reputation grew and the O'Malleys gathered wealth. But, as is well recorded, England, by the last decades of the sixteenth century was being established as a new nation state after its Reformation. Henry VIII had invested massively in a navy. Maritime expeditions had travelled far, and knowledge of the cosmopolitan extent of trade was opening and being understood. In this atmosphere, Grace and her fleet was becoming a thorn in the flesh for England's ambitions in Ireland. She married again, and this was to 'Iron Richard' Bourke. After this, the accommodation with the British establishment began, and a system called 'surrender and regrant', which allowed the Irish clans to be garnered into the English settlement plans, but then to have their status re-established so that they were Irish but also part of a developing system of organisation, which now began to stretch beyond the Dublin Pale and across the country. With hindsight, this can be seen as a very canny move on the part of the Tudors. It was a far better option than expanding military presence and spending huge investments in men and firepower. Robert Kee defines the nature of the surrender and regrant situation very neatly: 'A peaceful system of submission was offered to the Gaelic chiefs by which they could surrender their land to the King and immediately receive them back again, "regranted". In this way they acknowledged that her only title to the land they held was through the King.'

To see how the place of Grace O'Malley in Irish history became one of partly unstable narrative, reaching into the mythic proportions one would equally find in tales of Dick Turpin or Robin Hood, the place to look is in works spanning genres of popular topography and travel with a strand of history always present. In H.V. Morton's *In Search of Ireland*, he hints at his approach by quoting the Tudor chronicler Raphael Holinshed on the Emerald Isle: 'The people are thus inclined: religious, frank, amorous, sufferable of infinite pains, very glorious, many sorcerers, excellent horsemen, delighted with wars, great alms-givers, passing in hospitality.' He demonstrates these attitudes in writing of O'Malley. Writing of Clew Bay, he notes: 'On the shore facing the mainland is the ruined tower of Grace O'Malley's castle. Legend says that this remarkable Irishwomen was buried on the island in an abbey which now, like her stronghold, is a ruin.'

In telling the story, Morton includes supposed dialogues between Grace and Elizabeth, and this creates as much reality as a cartoon for children's entertainment. He cannot resist the kind of detail that would go well into some traditional storytelling as he ends his account of the pirate queen: 'But the story goes that in the nineteenth century a company was formed in Scotland for the acquisition of bones for manure. A ship was fitted out which raided the west of Ireland, where immense quantities of bones were piled up in churchyards and old abbeys. Grania's [Grace's] bones … went to manure Scottish acres.'

Grace was called by one commentator 'a nurse to all rebellions in Ireland' and obviously she would be a problem for Elizabeth and for Sir Richard Bingham, who was Lord President of Connacht. Bingham captured and jailed Grace's son, Tibbot, in Athlone, and there was a major problem for Grace, who was now officially Lady Bourke. Here, myth and legend enter the story. The handed-down tale is that Grace actually sailed to London and met the queen, to ask for her son's release. Whatever the circumstances, Elizabeth ordered Tibbot's release, and the rest of Grace's life was in what some would see as a compromise: as Anne Chambers, a specialist biographer in this case, wrote: 'fanciful tales' emerged about Grace. The facts are plain. The Privy Council acted as the queen wished, and life for the 'pirate queen' flattened into a retirement from her trade. Both she and Elizabeth died in 1603.

There had been the watershed Battle of Kinsale in 1601, which saw the defeat of Hugh O'Neill, Earl of Tyrone, and the famous 'flight of the earls' (O'Neill and the Earl of Tyrconnell). There was also a different kind of momentous event around this time: the foundation of the East India Company in 1599. Somehow the microcosmic events in Ireland were to lead to some very high-level strife for Britain, and the development of the Far East trade was to transform the whole world of Tudor and Stuart enterprise and business.

Then there is the business of smuggling in the sixteenth century, and of course there was interplay in the nexus of piracy, illicit goods and involvement in networks of the stealthy importation of banned goods. Naturally, there was always the kind of smuggling from wrecks, and indeed the nasty business of wrecking vessels in order to steal goods, but research has highlighted aspects of the subject rather more unknown, such as work by Dr Evan Jones into what is called 'white ruff crime' in Tudor Bristol. Dr Jones has revealed interesting material from accounting work. This was all about tax avoidance, and in the research, accounts records were studied alongside customs material. Topics included in the business were sometimes far more than plain food trading, and one of these was firearms. Made here, in the Forest of Dean, they surely would have been guarded and valued with some sense of method, but as Dr Jones learned, 'Bristol's merchants were far more concerned with their own pockets than the interests of the state.'

This kind of context of illicit misdeed in commerce needed informers, and such was the case of a certain Tegge Plowman in 1541, who did some observation and reporting for the crown on a merchant called Pryn. Plowman ran into trouble, but Pryn carried on as usual, at one point becoming sheriff of the city.

On a much larger scale, the men who worked as informers in this context could do very well financially and operate on a very wide scale of operation. Such a man figures in one of the Star Chamber stories collected by G.R. Elton. The person in question is George Whelplay, who saw rich opportunities in becoming an enforcer of the law rather than simply being a law breaker. He managed to bring no less a person than Thomas Cromwell into his enterprise, and it is clear that Whelplay had a group of assistants who supported him. He thus had permission, written in handwriting, from Cromwell when he arrived to swing into action. He could actually approach and board vessels and investigate. On one of his first forays into action, he and his men boarded a ship in the Solent which was in the process of smuggling gold bullion out of England, so his work started well.

However, Whelplay worked on a grand scale; he was ambitious, and always likely to offend someone or over step the line. He would have to fight in court, after complaints, and explain his actions and decisions. Elton explains how he worked:

> … he showed that he had confiscated certain goods or merchandise in some part of England which were being illegally exported, or which had been put up for sale in a public market although not made according to statutory specifications. Whelplay then prayed the court's decision and for himself the moiety of the value forfeited. These actions were started under statutes which arranged for the confiscation of the offending property rather than the imposition of a fixed fine; the principle that the informer took half still applied.

It can be seen here that though he may have become considerably rich, Whelplay made enemies. There are twenty bills surviving as being entered by Whelplay, and they are offences against proclamations, so this implies that he was always ready to act quickly, before anyone else. He became greedy and went too far. He informed against his friends, at the London haberdashers, and he was eventually beaten by the courts procedures, as his prosecution was moved to the Exchequer.

As Elton concludes, Whelplay's career as an informer shows what could be done to exploit a system that tried to work without the support of a police force, or any uniform and reliable methods of surveillance and regulation; Elton concludes with a statement about why there was a failure at the heart of the trade: 'In his way stood, on the one hand, the complicity of the local customs officials … on the other hand there were the stubborn local loyalties of assize juries who rated perjury very much lower in the scale of crime than the conviction of a local man on the word of a Londoner.'

One suspects that the great work on smuggling and piracy in this period is still waiting to be written, or is in progress. Various interested parties were always at work across Britain when it came to outside interference with local and regional organised crime. In fact, if the historian glances ahead to the eighteenth century, a focus on coastal patrol for smuggling reveals the strange and inefficient occupation of the riding officer, in which role the poor official had to patrol a lengthy part of our coasts alone, and was unable to act against wrongdoers without summoning the militia. It is no wonder that smuggling and piracy were always big business, and attractive to a large proportion of the lower classes.

Chapter 10

Criminal Tales and Bedside Reading

O! What men dare do! What men may do! What men daily do, not knowing what they do!

Shakespeare, *Much Ado About Nothing*

Put the focus on any period in history in which there is a print culture, and there will be stories; many of these stories will be about crime. Today we think of the representative eras of the true crime genre as being the age of the noose, primarily the Georgian years when the statute books were packed with capital offences. This age of Tyburn and public executions is arguably the most attractive to writers and film makers in mass media, and that age is followed closely by the Victorian, up to 1868 when public hangings stopped. Until that date a judicial execution was a very popular attraction, and crowds gathered. Yet this was simply a matter of a hangman and a noose, with a solemn procession of officials and dignitaries in line to accompany the condemned person to his or her end. It was a neck and a rope. The Tudors had much more to offer.

The images of Tudor executions offer more to the crowds who were hungry for a sight of extreme suffering and slow, agonising deaths could see women being burned, traitors being hanged, drawn and quartered, and convicts being dragged on hurdles to their appointment with the hangman. The Georgians could offer the attractive and desperate last dying speech and hopefully a sad rejection of the felon's sins and crimes which led to the scaffold. But the Tudors, and also the Stuarts, had the axe. What a crime out in public offered was a death march and a humiliation as a prelude to the gore.

The Georgian and Victorian eras had a much more substantial literature of crime, when it came to the media exploiting the tales of notorious villains, and as well as narratives by 'ordinaries' (the prison warders) which sold at printer's places, there were the cheap broadsides and journals, hawkers' compilations, and stories of sinners in religious printings. What, in contrast, did the Tudors have for their true crime reads? Some of the writings about crime by scribes in the Tudor and Stuart years are inanely ridiculous, and suggest that readers who wanted narratives on crime and law could take a wide spectrum of reading options, such as one book from 1642 by Mario Bettinus, which gives advice on escaping from prison using a drawing of a man using a mirror. Bettinus wrote: '… you see in the figure on the right that the prisoner (a) secretly secures liberty for himself as he points the lens (b) toward the sun, and liquefies the lead joints (c) with which the iron bars are fastened outside the walls so that he may freely escape …'

Far more entertaining for those drawn to true crime was what Shakespeare had to offer in *Othello*, for instance, which is a gripping tale of jealousy and murder. *Othello* is a tragedy, and such stories had usually been accounts of powerful figures in history, brought down to ruin by their sins, aspirations and dark emotions in a world of danger and fragility – such men as Julius Caesar, King Lear or Macbeth. But Othello (1604), although a general working for the Venetian republic, is on stage primarily as a husband, with his wife, Desdemona, and his nasty so-called 'ancient' or chief military batman, Iago. Intense jealousy, perilous unreason and a dagger lead to a murder within the home. What the Bard had produced was a domestic drama, and that takes the modern reader closer to what we call true crime.

An interchange between Othello and Lodovico, not long before Othello is taken away for punishment, has much the same interest we find in murder scenes down the years:

> Lodovico: O thou Othello, that wert once so good,
> fallen in the practice of a damned slave,
> what should be said of thee?
> Othello: Why anything.
> An honourable murderer if you will:
> but nought I did in hate, but all in honour.

The question of what should be said of Othello invites an explanation, and so the Elizabethan playgoer is offered two abstractions to consider. Was there anything honourable about a man stabbing his wife? Was there an act of hatred before the audience? Is Othello deluded?

This genre of drama became popular, and presented murder at home, where Agatha Christie often placed it. The Elizabethan and early Stuart period saw the rise of plays under the heading of domestic dramas. An example of the genre that slots neatly into true crime thinking and writing is the woeful tale of Walter Calverley.

In 1608, the play *A Yorkshire Tragedy* was published and was printed as being written by William Shakespeare. Scholarship since then has shown that it was almost certainly not written by him. The story is in the popular Elizabethan genre of the domestic tragedy, and it is based on events at Calverley Hall, near Bradford, in 1605. These 'events' were a horrendous and bloody murder by a father of his own sons. He also stabbed his poor wife. It was a story with the same kind of melodramatic appeal as the Victorian sensation trial – full of violent rage and senseless blood spilling, the work of a madman. It matched well with the current popularity of nasty and deranged Machiavellian revenge drama. But there was nothing melodramatic about the real events, and the killer in question has to rank as one of the very worst Bradford villains.

That was the one important difference between the literary tale and the story itself: the events really did happen, and to a family with links to some of the mightiest people in the land. The killer, Walter Calverley, had married Philippa Brooke in 1599. She was a member of the Brooke family who included no less a person than Sir Robert Cecil; Philippa was Cecil's aunt. Cecil became Secretary of State in 1596, and held onto power for a considerable time by the standards of the Elizabethan period, still being a key man in James I's government (he was called 'the little beagle' by the king).

What actually happened that awful day in April 1605 we will almost certainly never know. Walter had been in severe trouble with his mounting debts; he had been selling off much of his extensive land in the East Riding, as well as property in Pudsey, Burley and Menston. In fact, the couple had only been married for a year when the new husband was imprisoned for debt and was very ill. His mother-in-law had described him as 'unstayed' (unstable). There was a history of insanity in his family. His father, William, was undoubtedly a lunatic; he was a fervent Catholic at a time when that could have cost him his life. In 1569 the Catholics in the north had risen against the monarch and the reprisals when that failed were savage in the extreme. Walter was also imprisoned at one time in London, for making speeches of a seditious nature in public. He died young, just 39. The man had massive fines imposed on him for absence from church, so the political and legal pressures were tight. It seems quite amazing that the Brookes allowed his son's marriage into their ranks at all.

The pressures from debt, religious belief and those of marriage into a powerful family no doubt weighed heavily on Walter. It would have all gone down very hard; the family could trace its origins to around 1100 when the Calverleys had come south from Scotland, and the place name Calverley is mentioned in the *Domesday Book* of 1086 (meaning a place where calves are pastured). That spring, Walter snapped; there had been a catalyst, since there had been a notable witch trial in the area, just a month before he went into his rage. Locals had been spoken of with suspicion by their neighbours; it was all turning nasty.

What was there left for Calverley and his sons? His mind must have thought that death would release the boys from a life of penury and suffering. To make matters worse (and here we must read between the lines) his own mother, Katherine, who had lands around Burton Agnes, was buying more land and her wealth grew. She had said that she was not intending to leave any of this wealth to her stressed and unbalanced son.

The details we have of what happened at the hall come from a pamphlet published just a few weeks after the murders. Strangely, other legal documentation has not survived, and that seems to be rather more than coincidence when we realise that the Brookes were in bigger trouble: Lord Brooke was a friend of Sir Walter Raleigh, and he followed him into disgrace, being reprieved by James I in December 1603. Raleigh was shut in the Tower of London on a charge of treason and was executed in 1618. The new king was looking for a 'good press' on his arrival from the north, and Brooke's connections there may have saved him, whereas Raleigh had made enemies at court.

We rely for the narrative, then, on the pamphlet. This has Walter as a man under pressure from the start: a man ranting about his wife's infidelity. Then troubles come thick and fast, such as a report that his brother is in gaol, and that is the last straw for him. One poor son comes on stage with a whip and top and is promptly stabbed. Then he loses control totally and raves into his wife's room. In a desperate struggle as his wife tries to fight him off the children, Walter stabs the other boy, and then his wife. She falls down wounded and Walter runs to find the other son, who is also wounded. The language is equal to any popular thriller:

> Husband: Comest thou between my fury to question me?
> Servant: Were you the Devil I would hold you Sir.
> Husband: Hold me? Presumption, I'll undo thee for it!
> Servant: Sblood! You have undone us all, Sir.

Walter is finally tracked down after he has run away in a rage, then dragged before a magistrate and taken to Wakefield (not to York as there was a plague there at the time). But later he was moved to York and kept there until the next Assize. We know just two bare facts about the outcome. First, that Walter was pressed to death on 5 August, and buried on the same day; and that he was buried in the grounds of St Mary's. We think immediately of the death of Margaret Clitherow when we think of pressing as a method of execution: slow and barbarous in the extreme. The prisoner would be naked under a board and then stones would be gradually placed on the board to crush him to death.

Walter's wife married again, a few years later; she had three daughters, and she lived until 1613. Two entries in burial registers tell the hard facts of the Yorkshire tragedy: the first says simply, 'Calverley, St Wilfrid's 24 April 1605. Wllm and Walter, sons of Walter Calverley Esq'. The second is more explicit and powerful:

> York, St Mary's Castlegate 5 Aug. 1605
> Walter Calverley executed for murthering unnaturally
> Two of his own children the 23 April 1605
> Was buried the said 5 August.

A.C. Cawley, the literary scholar, points out the lingering fascination of the case. As he notes, Calverley's reasons for remaining mute at the trial 'are not clear at all'. Refusing to plead actually protected his land and stock because the assets were left in a trust, so they would not be lost when the owner committed a felony. A felony entailed the loss of all possessions, as a rule, so people searched for ways around that problem. Maybe Walter was much more canny than he seemed, and in control in some ways. A simpler solution, as Cawley suggests, is that 'he may have been seeking the speediest way to end his life'. If so, then he certainly succeeded.

The text of *A Yorkshire Tragedy* lies on the bookshelves in the English Literature section of the university libraries; maybe it gathers dust. But beneath that academic exterior lies one of the worst, most heart-rending murders in the history of the county. Far more often the subject of attention in studies of the drama of this period is the drama of Thomas Heywood. Long before *Othello*, this unknown author had written the play *Arden of Faversham* (1590) and this murder story ends with an epilogue that confirms its place in what has almost always figured in the true crime genre: adequate retribution of malevolence and facts about these things:

> Black Will was burnt in Flushing on a stage. Greene was hanged at Ospringe in Kent. The painter fled, and how he died we know not.

Heywood even adds the kind of solemn finality the genre likes:

> And in the grass his body's print was seen two years and more after the deed was done. Gentlemen, we hope you will pardon this naked tragedy.

The author shows here that he had a very sound knowledge of that special, intriguing sharing of a dark deed that true crime offers, with the morality seeping through the closure of the stories as sure as blood seeps through a body. It is as if Heywood has the instinct of the crime writer to know the more subtle reasons why readers and audiences are drawn to such tales.

Martin Wiggins, editor of Heywood and others, helpfully provides a list of the domestic dramas written between 1590 and the early Stuart years. These include three works by Heywood, and also plays that indicate by title the kind of experience awaiting the audience, such as George Wilkins's play *The Miseries of Enforced Marriage* (1606) and Robert Yarrington's *A Warning for Fair Women* (1598). Whoever was the writer behind the *Arden* play, he or she was breaking new ground, and was aware of the appeal of this kind of play. At the opening, there is a reference to the wealth acquired by Arden from the 1530s monasteries acquisition by the king: 'My gracious lord the Duke of Somerset/hath freely given to thee and to thy heirs/by letters patents from His Majesty/all the lands of the Abbey of Faversham'. This is contextual material alongside the kind of subversive emotional tangles in the human community that were to be Shakespeare's focus point:

> Love letters passed 'twixt Mosby and my wife,
> And they have privy meetings in the town.
> Nay, on his finger did I spy a ring
> Which at our marriage day the priest put on.
> Can any grief be so great as this?

The real test of such a play as a crime story, of course, is in the murder. The audience hears the report of the killing, and it is written with some sense of restraint. There has even been a high level of humour in the bungling and hesitation of the crooks Black Will and his accomplice, but the author is able to deliver the shock with a feeling for that sense of immediacy a murder tale must have:

> FRANKLIN: I fear me he was murdered in this house
> And carried to the fields, for from that place
> Backwards and forwards may you see
> The print of many feet within the snow,
> And look about this chamber where we are,
> And you shall find part of his guiltless blood

There were other genres of drama in the late Elizabethan and early Stuart period, notably the revenge tragedies of Webster and others, but in the domestic dramas we have something close to a situation in which an author includes that dimension of social dislocation and apprehension that touches on the chaos from immorality that the great Tudor intellectual Robert Hooker described in his tract on law:

'See we not plainly that obedience of creatures unto the law of nature is the way of the whole world?'

There was another dramatic genre that had an impact on the representations of real crime: the revenge tragedy. This makes productive use of the figure of the 'malcontent' and this stage figure fits neatly into the element in society at the time who is the centre of subversion and evil. L.G. Salingar pinpointed the importance of this revenge genre, which dealt in bloody vengeance against a restless and vicious individual:

> The theme of revenge … was popular in Elizabethan tragedy because it touched important questions of the day: the social problems of personal honour and the survival of feudal lawlessness; the political problem of tyranny and resistance; and the supreme question of providence, with it provocative contrasts between human vengeance and divine.

Salingar also notes the other elements in the revenge genre: 'scenes of madness, and macabre contrasts between death and revelry'. In these plays, exemplified in the classic works *The Revenger's Tragedy* by Cyril Tourneur and *The Spanish Tragedy* by Thomas Kyd, what is put on stage is a confrontation with a moral law, issues of outrageous violence and outrage. In short, we have the roots of one of the true crime genre's most representative ingredients: bloody suffering and man's inhumanity. Revenge deals with the lower, beastly elements in man, as described in the great chain of being. It also played on effective stereotypes, such as the Machiavellian villain, and that related to the saying expressed by moralists, 'the Italianate Englishman is the devil incarnate'. John Marston (1576–1634) wrote *The Malcontent* in 1604, and this illustrates the sociopathic sufferer of anomie as a character of deep interest in these crime stories. Salingar, in the same essay as quoted above, sums up Marston's character: 'He could stimulate others … but his own work is a tangle of unmastered emotions and undigested ideas …' Marston lectured at the Middle Temple and studied at Oxford, and as a dramatist, he found success in the last years of Elizabeth and in the succeeding dozen years or so. After that he took holy orders and had the living of Christchurch in Hampshire. He also wrote satires, and in some of the lines in these poems one may see the very core of his theme of creating a 'malcontent':

> Reason, by prudence in her function,
> had wont to tutor all our actions,
> aiding, with precepts of philosophy,
> our feebled nature's imbecility;
> but now affection, will concupiscence,
> have got o'er reason chief pre-eminence …

Standard accounts of revenge tragedy usually refer to the influence of Machiavelli, and the meanings of the adjective 'Machiavellian' applied to literary characters. Niccolo Machiavelli (1467–1527) certainly knew the kind of experience required in contexts of crime writing. In 1512 he was arrested, under the Medici regime, for his part in a plot, and he experienced the pains of the *strappado* punishment. In this, the victim's hands were tied behind his back, pulled up to a beam, and then dropped with force. We can barely imagine the pain involved. Poor Machiavelli somehow survived and became a writer after his release in 1513. After the impact of his classic work of political power, *The Prince*, his name and influence spread, and his interest in how a state can be subject to moral decay certainly provided interest as well as literary themes to many. Vincent Cronin, writing on the Italian renaissance, writes in his profile of the man something that explains the myth as well as the personality:

> Machiavelli's prince is one who has come to absolute power by his own ability. To retain power, he must

> have a strong army, lead it himself in the field, and treat every other state as a potential enemy. Such a man, says Machiavelli, may practise deliberate cruelty, deceit, treachery, even murder, and he should appeal always to men's fear rather than to their respect. 'The end justifies the means, if the end be good' where *good* means effective.

In John Webster's work there is a strange, compelling element of tormented subversion. Thirty years ago it appeared to be enough, in literary commentaries, to explain Machiavelli as the source of these malcontent characters, but there is no doubt that many of the stage confrontations and clashes, inner turmoil and subversion relate powerfully to the kind of themes readers of true crime enjoy. These words of Cornelia, for instance, in *The White Devil*, present this Gothic setting:

> Call for the robin redbreast and the wren
> Since over shady groves they hover,
> And with leaves and flowers do cover
> The friendless bodies of unburied men …
> But keep the wolf from hence, that's foe to men,
> For with his nails he'll dig them up again.

The White Devil has enough dramatic and shocking material to please the most devoted true crime enthusiast. The Machiavellian figure Flamineo helps the Duke of Brachiano to achieve his various unpleasant aims in life, and the play includes poisoning, murder, and a very powerful trial episode. Murder piles upon murder, and at the centre is the character of Vittoria, who certainly suffers at the heart of all the incident and bloody opposition.

John Webster, the dramatist (1578–1632), was also a coachmaker in London. He is best known for *The Duchess of Malfi* (*c.*1609) and there have been high claims for his ability. Margaret Drabble, in her reference work on literature, notes that with his tragedies: 'Webster has achieved a reputation second only to Shakespeare's; they have been revived in this century more frequently than those of any other of Shakespeare's contemporaries.' The other producers of some of the key revenge plays are not so well remembered, but Marston's *The Malcontent*, published in 1604, has possibly the most brash and raw dissenting and threatening restless spirit in the Duke of Genoa, who is disguised as the malcontent, and his name is far from being subtle or restrained: Malvole.

What accounts for the success of the revenge plays is the depth and passionate rage in the inner motivations of the evildoers. As with later true crime literature, much of the interest for reader or for audience is the explanations of motivation for the criminal acts, because of course, the readers and watchers of the tales will relate the motivations to real life and its trials, challenges and sufferings.

Going back to Marlowe and his stage figures Faustus and Tamburlaine, a similar kind of violence and shock fills the stage, but the references in the setting are global rather than interior.

The theatre, in the works of the authors of revenge tragedy, and the domestic tragedy, certainly catered for the dark humour and sick, tainted themes of what was in many ways Gothic, long before the era we associate with that genre in vampire literature and film; but the Machiavellian character is speaking from the margins of moral society, of the safe conformity, supposedly maintained by the tough law of repression around the dramatists as they worked. It was, after all, a perilous world to be living in, between the Armada and the death of Elizabeth. There was always talk of plots and rumours of rebellion. This was a new nation state, re-established in a sense since 1534 and that Act of Uniformity, 'going it alone' in a European world of Christendom. There was a Holy Roman Empire, and there was the powerful Spanish state with its expanding New World empire. There was little England, on the edge of that world, with a succession of three more monarchs since the death of Henry VIII, the man who had transformed the world and the way a country's citizens were supposed to relate to their God.

In this context, the kinds of offences of the avengers, the antisocial souls at odds with established morality, were anti-heroes against the grain. These dissenters from conformity were, as T.S. Eliot put it, eloquent in emotional inconsistence. They showed 'an internal incoherence of feelings' – and this is at the core of so much in true crime writing.

Then there is the literature of crime, as read by the general population. Some of the titles a century after the Tudors in this category shows how the print trade in true crime progressed. These are some of the popular chap books of the years between *c.*1670 and 1740:

> *The Bloody Tragedy*, or a dreadful warning to disobedient children.
> *A Pious Exhortation* delivered in a prison by an innocent sufferer.
> *The Village Tragedy, or Murder Upon Murder*, written against seduction so fatal a few weeks ago by a young woman near York.
> *Pathetic Sufferings of Louise Harwood* who was seduced by Lieutenant Harris.

These chap books are linked by name to the old occupation of the chapman, and appeared mainly in the early seventeenth century. John Ashton, writing in 1882, in an anthology of these publications, summarises their origin:

> The chapman, too, is a thing of the past, although we still have hawkers and the travelling 'credit drapers' of tallymen, yet penetrate every village; but the chapman, as described by Cotsgrave in his Dictionary of the French

> and English Tongues (London, 1611) no longer exists. He is there faithfully portrayed under the heading 'Bissouart, a paltry pedlar, who in a long pack ormaund … hath almanacks, books of news, or other trifling ware to sell'.

Along with the biblical and folk tales came stories of transgression and menace, danger and moral instability such as *God's Judgement on All Blasphemers*; *The Whole Trial and Indictment of John Barleycorn*; *Knight; A True Tale of Robin Hood*; and *The Bloody Tragedy*. A typical example is the story of *John Gregg and His Family of Robbers and Murderers*, which is outstanding as material relating to the commercial hyperbole of the most blatant of true crime promotion. The robbers are described in this way:

> Who took up their abode in a cave near to the sea side in Clovaley in Devonshire, where they lived twenty-five years without so much as once going to visit any city or town. How they robbed above one thousand persons and ate all they robbed. How at last they were happily discovered by a pack of blood hounds, and how John Gregg, his wife, eight sons, six daughters, eighteen grandsons and fourteen grand daughters were all seized and executed by being cast alive into fires, and were burnt.

Every feature of this relates to the story of Sawney Beane and family, who were cave-dwelling savages on the Galloway coast in the 1590s. James I actually led a small army to their lair. There were cadavers in the inner cave, which was found by the dogs of the Jacobean force. According to main sources, the male Beanes were subjected to their limbs being torn off, and all the clan were executed.

The final strand in the crime literature is the category dealing with 'coney catching', as it was known. A 'coney' means rabbit, but also, in the argot of the world of thieves and scammers, it signifies a dupe, or gull. In Shakespeare's *Othello*, Rodrigo is named as 'a Venetian gentleman' in the cast list, but is essentially a gull for the malevolent Iago, who cajoles him and leads him on with false information and promises, all the while milking him of his money. We see the steady progress of Iago's machinations; but the coney catching genre of writing known by some today as 'a Tudor craze' was based on work by Robert Greene (1558–92) of Norwich.

Historians and commentators tend to stress the difficulty of establishing any hard facts about Greene. Reading summaries of his life becomes an experience of a subject constantly slipping away from any certainty. He was 'probably' various identities. He did become a Cambridge scholar, gaining his BA in 1580 and then he transferred to a different college to take his MA in 1583. Then he became a literary man, writing in a number of genres, and there is a claim that he was the first professional writer in our literature, Chaucer, the 'father of English poetry' and Caedmon (*fl.* 670) of Northumbria not being full-time professionals in literature. Whatever the facts, we do know that Greene's collection of short works on the work of the criminal community of Tudor England were very successful. Equally, Thomas Harman published a work of wide influence, called *The Groundwork of Conny-Catching* [*sic*] in 1592. Greene and Harman achieved commercial success in the category of what we would now consider to be underworld confessional writing. In terms of twentieth-century crime writing, they provide something similar to a confessional memoir by a former con, such as the books by Frankie Fraser on his gangland and prison experience.

The coney catching tales are all about the tricks of the criminal trades. In his book *Life in Shakespeare's England*, scholar and Elizabethan specialist historian John Dover Wilson builds his portrait of late Tudor life around themes illustrated from the Bard and other writers. In his profile of crimes, coney catching is placed as the most fruitful source for this. Anyone wanting to know the tricks of any nefarious illegal trade would buy Greene's work and enjoy a description of the *modus operandi* of a villain. This was all in a culture of exploitation wherever communities gathered. For instance, the 'hooker or angler' worked in this way:

> For them customably [*sic*] carry with them a staff of five or six feet long, in which, within one inch of the top thereof, is a little hole bored through, in which hole they put an iron hook, and with the same they will pluck unto them quickly anything that they may reach therewith, which hook in the daytime they covertly carry about them, and is never seen or taken out till they come to the place where they work their feat.

Dover Wilson provides a guide to the various criminal occupations, as written in a work by William Harrison in 1587, and this includes fourteen male and nine female terms for specific skills or definitions of their work.

Harrison is also one of the most explicit and expressive authors of another variety of crime writing: the fascination with prison and physical punishment. His book includes vivid accounts of what might happen to a rogue who has been caught and convicted, after a spell in gaol: '… he is then immediately adjudged to be grievously whipped and burned through the gristle of the right ear with a hot iron of the compass of an inch about, as a manifestation of a wicked life … and this judgement is to be executed upon him unless some honest person worth five pounds … will be bound … to retain him.'

This reveals an important aspect of crime and punishment at this time: the need for public shaming. This was hardly a new presence in the law. In 1925, for instance, Mr Edward O'Toole, a schoolmaster, stood in the dock at the Old Bailey charged with slander. He was open to the assaults of journalism and the ruin of his reputation. A woman had had his child, outside wedlock. Simply to appear where he did, and for the events to feature in *The Times*, was ruin. A century later, *The Daily Telegraph* reported that 'the right to offend is part of free speech' after a man had been tried for shouting an offensive phrase in public against Islam. The concluding paragraph of *The Telegraph* report quotes the judge: 'Today's decision reaffirms the vital principle that free speech protects the right to offend, shock or disturb, even when it challenges deeply held religious beliefs.'

Both cases illustrate the spectrum of moral/legal issues at law *c*.1590: the former would have been entirely understood by the Elizabethans, and the latter would read like impossible science fiction.

The theme here is all about public knowledge of acts of speech or expression of belief. Built into the conception of suitable punishment was the mindset that insisted upon displaying criminals in public – in stocks or pillory mainly, but also walking at the end of a cart. This kind of act was later very much related to the notion of 'rough music' in which offenders against public decency (such as fornicators) were harassed and insulted, their names bruited about the streets, as a punishment from custom rather than from a magistrate. Ruth Goodman has shown, in her book, *How to Behave Badly in Renaissance Britain*, how significant the behaviour relating to mockery, gestures and offensive speech was to the Tudors and Stuarts. She wrote about mockery and parody, that: 'Many a parishioner, riled by the contents of a sermon … relieved their feelings with a mockery … Thomas Nashe in 1595 describes hypocritical Puritans that "have Bibles always in their bosom" and are "heaving up their eyes to heaven".'

Clothes and appearance as indicators of faults, vices and shortcomings had been of another very old print tradition – the emblem book. These publications, as John Hordern explains: 'Are, fundamentally, picture books consisting of symbolic pictures accompanied by passages of prose or verse interpreting the picture and pointing to its moral lesson.' The first such work ever published was in Italy in 1531, *Emblematum Liber* by Andrea Alciati. How these linked to crime stories is interesting.

They pointed morals via depictions and texts of unacceptable or sinful behaviour, such as in Cesare Ripa's *Ripa's Iconologia* of 1593. Again, Hordern describes the nature of these images: 'Truth is presented as a naked women staring at the sun, holding a book and a branch of palm, and treading down the world from her foot.' He adds that in Jacobean England, writers turned to *Iconologia* 'for details of the costume and accoutrements proper to the personification of vices, virtues, emotions and the like …'

Appearance, public image and reputation were fundamental to Tudor community and belonging, and crime stories made much of this. Once again, Shakespeare provides one of the clearest examples in the character of one of his greatest comic creations, Sir John Falstaff, in *Henry IV Part I*:

> A certain Lord, neat, and trimly dressed fresh as a bridegroom; and his chin new reaped, showed like a stubble land at harvest home. He was perfumed like a milliner and twixt his finger and his thumb he held a pouncet-box, which ever and anon he gave it his nose and took 't away again.

True crime writing has always put the focus on the revelatory aspect of the subject, taking the stance of showing the reader an unfamiliar world and the lives of transgression within the readers' society. Yet in the sixteenth century this material for creative writing, in all popular genres, was just opening out. The revenge dramas and murder stories based on fact cornered the market in tense, subversive experience of people breaking the mould of conformity and social behaviour, but there is no doubt that Robert Greene, the all-round author, made a name for himself as a ground-breaker. He did not have a long life, and what he wrote about himself is not necessarily based on fact; he wrote a work called *The Repentance of Robert Greene*, and he wrote about European journeys, but even these are not verified. What does appear to be true is the account of his death as explained by Edward Lucie-Smith:

> His excesses, and his final repentance on his miserable death bed, were copiously written up by himself and others (we learn that his death was caused by a fatal banquet of Rhenish wine and pickled herring). Greene's talent is slight but strangely mixed – it combines the pastoral, the realistic and the moralising.

A case before the Court of Chivalry slightly outside the Tudor span of years but relevant to this theme, is that of Dowman v Faulcon in 1639, which illustrates exactly the issue of insult and mockery. It happened in Stamford, Lincolnshire, at the open fair. The court report states: 'Before divers gentlemen of good fashion and quality. Dowman claimed that Faucon had insulted him. Faucon gave him the lie in a disgraceful and angry manner, calling him "Will, or William Dowman" without any addition at all belonging to him as a gentleman thereby intending to provoke him to a duel. Process was granted … but Dowman indicated to the Earl Marshal that the case had been settled.' It was surely a desirable outcome, avoiding the risk of a serious injury or a murder.

Duelling was certainly a speedy way to take a life or maim someone for life. The act of a duel was illegal in the view of the state, and of course, also of the church. It was a habit taken from Italian culture, and as was commonly held as an opinion in this context, 'the Italianate Englishman is the devil incarnate'. But duels happened, and they were an attractive proposition to the kind of restless and touchy blades Shakespeare depicts in *Romeo and Juliet*. Men keenly learned to fence and use the deadly weapon of the rapier, as described in the foregoing account of the fights in the theatrical communities. We see on stage the beginning of a fight between the Montague and Capulet men with the words, 'No, Sir, I do not bite my thumb at you;

but I bite my thumb Sir,' and in *As You Like It*, Shakespeare gives us the full and vain ritual of the build-up of insults and responses when a fight is imminent.

The comic character Touchstone has the words in his satirical speech:

> the first, the retort courteous; the second, the quip modest; the third, the reply churlish; the fourth, the reproof valiant; the fifth, the countercheck quarrelsome; the sixth, the lie with circumstance; the seventh, the lie direct.

The bestseller, for young gentlemen in search of a fight, was *His Practise, in Two Bookes* by Vincentio Saviolo. The two-part work's contents are advertised as 'The first intreating of the use of the rapier and dagger. The second of honor and honourable quarrels', and was printed in 1595.

Ruth Goodman, in her account of Tudor bad manners, refers to a duel at Rye between John Wollfe and John Peerse, who wanted 'to see themselves as potential gentlemen of honour'. Peerse was convicted of manslaughter after, as Goodman puts it, 'killing his adversary with what appears to have been a thrust that severed the femoral artery, John Wollfe dying immediately …'

For the most extreme form of a duel, the focus has to be on the earlier history: duelling became a way of sorting out a private quarrel. A reference work summarises what happened in France: 'It had grown to such an extent, and so many men of noble birth had been slain, that in 1626 Richelieu confiscated the property of duellists and banished them from France. In England, the popularity of duels really came after the Restoration in the 1660s.

Robert Chambers, the Scottish historian, in *Traditions of Edinburgh*, describes what happens when disagreements between men reach the explosive point a deathly confrontation without even the ritual of a duel. He explains the start of a fight between James

Johnson and a member of the Somerville family in 1596 after an insult was spoken:

> [Johnson] … with his sword drawn … marches up with his sword drawn, crying 'Turn, villain' he cuts Somerville in the head a deep and sore wound, the foulest stroke that ever Johnson was known to give … and much regretted afterwards by himself … Thus they continued near a quarter of an hour, clearing the callsay [causeway] so that in all the street Bow there was not one to be seen without their shop doors, neither durst any man attempt to red them [advise, call out to them] …

The result was an affray: others joined in. In this way was what was to become a *Newgate Calendar* standard criminal tale, the duel death, became a popular branch of true crime literature later on. In *The Newgate Calendar* of the 1820s, for instance, there is the story of 'Richard Thornhill, Convicted of Manslaughter, in Killing Sir Cholmondeley Deering, in a Duel'. Thornhill was hanged in 1711. The *Calendar* feature expresses the paradox of the crime very strongly: 'The abhorred and sanguinary practice of duelling offers to the offers to the reader, in the influence it is thought to have over strong and enlightened minds, a paradox most bewildering and humiliating.'

If one adjusts the span of interest in the criminal subjects for bedtime reading and stage shows, to focus only on sensation, then the drama is where the subjects explored were most powerful on audience involvement, because the ordinary Elizabethans would have known the feeling of living in a world with menace and apprehension in the stuff of everyday working life, and they would have also seen the wavering, unreliable nature of the laws they were supposed to follow and toe the line, when the line was always moving.

Some Conclusions

One of the greatest delusions of this world
is the hope that the evils of this world
can be cured by legislation.

Thomas Reed

The dominant thought accruing as the writing of this book progressed may be expressed in this way: so much coastline and so little there to defend it. Napoleon and Hitler must have thought the same in their time. Britain seems so fragile when you look at the Tudor map, and yet, in 1520, at the Field of the Cloth of Gold, Henry VIII tried to behave like the other European princes and potentates around him. We have to surmise that he contemplated the future strength and success of his navy as he was conceiving it at the time. Overall, my conclusions hinge on this sense of law trying to cope when all the while the lawmakers saw how easy it was to incite the next in a long line of rebellions, and they must have seen just how much violent crime was actively before them as they tried to steady the ship of state.

There are several thoughts and reflections emerging from a survey of the Tudor years that come to mind at the close of a project. Personally, the events between the accession of Henry VII in 1485 and the first actions on his son's maturity when regnant reinforce the aftermath of the previous century, which was primarily a time of war both with France and with the factions at home involved in the Wars of the Roses. One of the most well-informed historians of the wars in France, Jonathan Sumption, points out that there were extreme effects here, across the nation: 'The struggle came as close to total war as any before the twentieth century. The armies and fleets engaged were small by modern standards, but measured against a total English population of between 2 million and 2.5 million, of whom perhaps a third were able-bodied males, the wars must have occupied up to a tenth of England's available manpower.' Sumption also points out that the last campaigns of that war 'were essentially nothing more than demands for money with menaces'. The crisis in macroeconomics facing Henry VII was one reason behind his emphasis on gathering cash and resources, at the expense of so much else in law and administration which might have eventually helped Henry VIII in his ambitions for his nation and its reformation.

The other striking feature of those years of Henry VII was the reverberation across regions, allegiances and families after Bosworth. A battle for national supremacy that relates to an overall picture of a land fractured, divided and in many ways adrift will arguably be open to anarchy or civil war, and the wars of the Yorkists and Lancastrians has always been narrated as if there was no more than two belligerent groups thinking of nothing but the next confrontation. But such aspects of rule as the supervision of the marches and northern borders, and the party factions of rich aristocratic families were rooted, and always likely to rattle into action, as was the case in 1569 and in 1549, to say nothing of the revolts after the religious houses were grabbed and ruined.

A century before the Tudors, affairs of murder and manslaughter were relatively straightforward in court. But the process had its complications, as in this case from Norfolk:

> Richard Quynchard of Blythburgh and Geoffrey Chaloner, approvers, appealed Geoffrey ate Bush of Brampton for killing Thomas son on John Spark of Yelverton at Trowse … and for robbing two foreigners of cloth and

> goods worth 8s. Geoffrey comes and says that he wishes to defend himself in a duel. Richard the approver, claims that because he is missing two fingers … he cannot duel. Geoffrey ate Bush then puts him on the country. The jurors acquit him. Richard is hanged for false appeal. His chattels are nothing. Chaloner withdrew his appeal and was hanged. His chattels were nothing.

The approvers, which means the men who accused others in order to be acquitted of their indictment, both were hanged in the end after putting their case to a jury ('on the country') and this happened simply because their accused refused a duel. In other words, Richard and Chaloner were indicted of a felony, looked for a duel as a means of escape, and failed. Their backs were to the wall, and a fight was their best option. Geoffrey ate Bush wanted no fight. Everything was physical, raw, on the front foot, and the gallows awaited the weak or the unfortunate. Reading such a report, a comparison with a similar Tudor trial concludes that there may have been a similar simple process *c*.1500, but it was more a matter of words than deeds. The other noticeable feature of *c*.1390 is the absence of lawyers. This happened in a plain criminal activity of an attack and robbery on two strangers. Murder in the highways was common and outlaws abounded.

The concept of the outlaw was key in the case because in the mid to late fourteenth century outlaws were more on a grand scale than the Tudors faced. Tony Robinson, in his account of outlaws, describes the Folville gang: 'A generation after their deaths, the Folvilles were celebrated as the kind of outlaws who righted wrongs.' They had broken into a church and dragged the rector outside and beheaded him. The surprising fact here is that the victim was a Folville, and he was seen as the criminal who needed punishment – by the rest of his brotherhood. The outcome of this is that the Folville gang were, in effect, the 'law'.

The Tudor age may well have been a place where anyone with wealth was tentative at the least to go out and abroad, but at least the notion of a wild bunch-style gang was hard to achieve. The sixteenth century encouraged the formation of plenty of organised crime but it was largely stealthy, wary and underhand, a case of crimes in darkness and deceit. The case of Whelplay in my chapter on piracy shows also the importance of informers in a world in which no national or organised police structures were in existence.

One outstanding feature of the period regarding law is the extraordinary number of family stories from the aristocracy and elite or superior families across England. A survey of Tudor family stories soon reveals common occurrences, such as debt, imprisonment, legal confrontations, and even duels and affrays. The biography of one of the Crofts of Croft Castle in Herefordshire, Edward Croft, could be taken as typical. This is Edward Croft, who died in 1601. His father was arrested for 'questionable conduct in negotiations with the Duke of Parma' and something remarkable followed, as recounted in the History of Parliament Online: 'Croft, who blamed the Earl of Leicester, applied to a London conjuror, John Smith, to compass Leicester's death, which took place 4 Sept. Croft was charged with contriving his death but nothing is known of any trial.'

Croft himself was imprisoned for debt and eventually ran away to the Netherlands. As the family handbook for the Castle states, 'Edward was a reckless and perhaps unstable character … he was never allowed to inherit Croft which was put in trust for his son, Herbert.' This happened in a family that had provided the tutor for Prince Arthur, elder brother of Henry VIII, at Ludlow: the Croft in question was Sir Richard, who was at one time Treasurer of the Royal Household.

Such families would have probably enjoyed the literary and dramatic tragedies on the stage of their time, plays in which men were raised to a height of power and status and then experienced sharp and final decline, like Richard III in Shakespeare's pro-Tudor history play on the last of the Plantagenets. It was a literature of paranoia, with a mantra running something like 'kill your enemies, and also your potential ones'. The paranoia ran deep, like certain comparable eras in other locations of British history. The late Georgian years compare, with Napoleon over the water, amassing troops, and Dunkirk in 1940 with the possibility of an immense loss of life. But the Tudor paranoia was, one might argue, uniquely many sided.

One side of life was the steady obedience to the seasons, the church calendar and the responsibilities of tithes to the church and work on the vicar's glebe land; it was about community holding together with its own rules and safeguards. The other side of life was the bigger picture, out there, where things are done differently and where there are sovereigns and aristocrats, a world in which power is something men lust for and die for. Travel was perilous and had to be done in protective groups; pilgrimages made good sense, as there was strength in numbers. The individual had a responsibility to his family, his community and his sovereign, but under the Tudors, the monarch's presence on the margins of life must have seemed like nothing more than a voice giving orders and expressing fears.

Studying the Tudor state after the 1530s suggests that the situation for the English citizen was very much what we find in some later polities led by dictators. These leaders have the attitude of the 'proclamation'. This, a favourite of the Tudor monarchs, is no more than a public notice of a monarchical attitude or opinion. It has the colour of being a firmly held wish but could be little more than an expression of a negative mood after the recognition of a problem in society. I have to repeat here the point made in Chapter 1 about proclamations: the great legal historian, F.W. Maitland, explained the short-lived statute of 1539 – one Maitland called the most extraordinary act in the statute book – in this way. He wrote, 'it gave power to the King to make proclamations which should have the force of statutes; the punishment for disobedience might be fine or unlimited imprisonment. It was not to extend to life, limb or forfeiture.' Some folk might have thought of this as rule by bad temper or whim.

The bare facts of Tudor rule and the need for repressive laws lies in the fragile strength of the king or queen and their courts and immediate circles. As one knows generally from popular film and literature, it was a society in which a man could rise in the hierarchy of power and status by a combination of political acumen and toadying. The culture of sinecures and preference was still going strong in the Victorian years. Thomas Wolsey defines this image, and the fate of the Boleyns confirms the tragic pattern of rise – have power – decline – fall. But in effect the fragility of the establishment of rule was always evident in a state with no regular army or police force. Across the land there were constables, *poursuivants*, and most important of all for security, there were the militia lying in wait, supposedly ready to arm and support the monarch and his parliament. In reality, so much still depended on the nobles and their own levies.

In such a state, Machiavelli's advice would be respected, but we have to wonder that they did not heed this from the Italian master of power politics:

> A ruler who inherits power has less reason to need to upset his subjects than a new one and as a result is better loved. If he doesn't go out of his way to get himself hated, it's reasonable to suppose his people will wish him well. When a dynasty survives for generations memories fade and likewise motives for change, upheaval, on the contrary, always leaves the scaffolding for building further change.

Henry VIII was one of history's great masters of creating upheaval, and never understood that resistance to rapid change will be a foundation for both inner discontent and of public disorder.

As a historian of crime and transgression, I see in the Tudor methods of rule a complete ignorance and misunderstanding of the average man and woman in their realm. Their economy was ruled by staples such as wool and basic manufacturing commodities; it relied on hard labour, the demands of the seasons and local communal power under royal guidance. Yet that royal guidance was rooted at such a distance, and across the shires, people would have known their sovereign Henry, for instance, by the reports of his latest ceremonial mobile court, traversing the land to visit and exploit the ambitions of the local lords and ladies. The real rule was more of the nature, to use a modern metaphor, of an express train dashing through the country, glimpsed in a blur, than a stately carriage with hand-waving and chatty conversations with old folk and children.

This Tudor state was also one in which there were mercenaries or servants used in a way more reminiscent of a mafia outfit than a nation state with world ambitions. By the early Stuarts, this state would have some of its citizens living in America, and would be starting trade with the Far East. At home, as some of the Star Chamber records show, control of shipping, coastal trade and large-scale export and import transactions depended on a network of invisible and sometimes questionable franchise-like established practice. There were leaks in all the systems, opening up common practice to exploitation and corruption.

Above all this, where the real work was done, it was a culture of ascendency and aspiration run wild. Serving men served the serving men, and authority had a potent mix of promise and dismay, achievement and rejection. This culture was fixated on appearance, and the hints about this are not only in the causes of duels, but also in fashion, keeping face and holding on to one's place in one of the micro-cultures around the court centre.

The fashion followed this need for ostentation and display. Jane Malcolm-Davies, describing Tudor dress, wrote that the 'interplay of function, culture and style' was all about being 'dedicated followers of fashion' and the art of the time is informative on this. Images of social groups of people of high status show elaborate doublets, stockings and trimmings, with everything having an element of show and display. There is a very informative dimension of figure and pose in collective images. How one looks was eminently important, informing the watcher or counterpart in conversation about who you were and what you had in your place as defined by social practice.

For the reasons above relating to the need for society to 'work' in the sense of functioning without too much fear of the law and custom becoming hurdles to success, at the very heart of this life was an individual's faith, and in medieval Christendom the fear of death had its counter-argument in the reasoning about the pleasures of life on or near the land, nature's bounty at the core. Heads turning to the Pope and Rome were, with the English Reformation, asked to look elsewhere for certainty, and where they looked for reassurance they surely saw only coercion and commands. So much was ordered and so little was given. Where was affection, the love of community, the sharing of the rewards and securities of custom, then? It was still there in the room nearest to them in the great mansion of law, whose furthest reaches – in London – visited their area three times a year in the assizes, and there they would glimpse important judges and see justice done by the rope or the house of correction. Crime and law for the ordinary Tudors, then, was a mix of suppression and resistance: the fear and faith their forebears would have known, but with the possibility of pardons, rewards in heaven, and guidance from the pulpit which was of the same hue as spoken in London as in Newcastle or Worcester.

A Glossary of Technical and Legal Terms

Assizes

The story of the assize courts is a reflection of how the criminal law gradually developed and found a system that would have parity across the land. The courts represent the boldest step by which central legal power began to cover the king's domains, using the local and the national elements together. In each shire, the sheriff, who had been there since very early times, gathered the jury and the other machinery of law, ready for the visit of the assize judges, because that is what assizes were – courts done in transit – giving the assize towns distinguished visitors and a high level of ritual and importance for a few days each year.

Originally, the law courts followed the king, and his own court was the *Curia Regis.* Then in Magna Carta (1215) there was this sentence: 'Common pleas shall not follow our Court but shall be held in some certain place.' The result was that Westminster was made that 'place' but then the notion of having the top judges moving around to deal with criminal and civil cases became a workable option, with economic and logistical benefits, of course, as persons accused would be retained and then tried mostly in their own counties or provinces.

Since early medieval times, there had been assizes – literally 'sittings together' – to try causes and to gather officials in the English regions to compile enquiries and inventories into local possessions and actions. These were 'eyres' of assize, but they were not courts. The assize courts came when travelling justices went out into the counties to try cases:

the Assize of Clarendon in 1166 and the Council of Northampton in 1196 decreed that the country should be split into six areas in which the judges of the High Court would sit. These became known as circuits.

In Edward I's reign an act was passed to create court hearings in the local place of jury trial, before a summons for the jury to go to Westminster. The people involved were to come to London unless the trial had happened before: in Latin *nisi prius* (unless before). What developed over the centuries was that serious offences, crimes needing an indictment, had to be tried before a jury. The less-serious offences, summary ones, could be tried by a magistrate. In addition to that, the terms 'felony' and 'misdemeanour' also existed until they were abolished in 1967: a felony was a crime in which guilt would mean a forfeiture of possessions and land, so the offender's children would lose their inheritance. A misdemeanour was a less-serious crime.

The justices of assize had a number of powers. First, they had a commission of *oyer and terminer* (to listen and to act) on serious cases such as treason, murder, and any crime that was labelled a felony. They also had to try all people who had been charged and who had been languishing in gaol since their arrest, and they tried cases *nisi prius. Nisi prius* meant that a sheriff had to bring a case to London *unless before* (the Latin meaning) the assizes happened.

The assize circuits became established as the Home, Midland, Norfolk, Oxford, Eastern, Western and Northern, and the records for these run from 1558 to either 1864 or 1876, when assizes were reorganised, or to 1971, when the assizes were abolished and crown courts created. From the beginning, the assize circuits covered all counties except Cheshire, Durham, Lancashire and Middlesex, the first three being referred to as the Palatinate Courts. In 1876, some courts moved from one circuit to another.

The result of all this means that a criminal ancestor who committed a crime in Leeds, for instance, after 1876, would be tried in Leeds rather than in York, the former seat of an assize for the West Riding. The family historian needs to access the location of the court and trial as a first step.

A useful source for checking on which assizes were on the circuit at any time between the late eighteenth century and the end of the nineteenth is to look at *The Gentleman's Magazine*, which listed assizes and names of judges presiding at each one. This journal appeared annually. The assizes were held twice a year, from the thirteenth century until they ended in 1971, and these sessions were referred to as Spring and Winter. A third session could be held at times if the gaols were full – as in times of popular revolt and riots, or activities by gangs.

The assizes were divided into two areas: for civil cases, referred to as 'crown' – and criminal cases. Two judges would be on the road, each with a responsibility for one of the two areas of law. In the law reports in *The Times*, these are marked clearly, in capitals. For instance, for the Winter Assizes in York in December 1844, we have:

> WINTER ASSIZES
> NORTHERN CIRCUIT
> YORK, DECEMBER 5.
> (Before Mr Justice Coleridge)
> The newspapers tended to use the terms, 'Crown side' and 'criminal side'.

Attainder

This is the withdrawal of a person's civil rights, coming from a conviction of high treason. 'In these cases goods, lands, titles and armorial bearings of an attainted person could not be inherited by his heirs until the attainder had been revoked.' Stephen Friar in *The Sutton Companion to Local History.*

Benefit of Clergy

Originally, this was a claim from clergymen that they were outside the legal process of the state courts, and must be tried by a church court. Under the Tudors this became a serious issue for the state, as the privilege was extended into secular trials.

Borsholder
The head of a tithing.

Bridewell/House of Correction
The Bridewell in London that gave the name to the first houses of correction was built between 1515 and 1523, at a cost of £25,000. In 1556 it was defined as a hospital, and it was managed by the same people who ran Bethlehem hospital. It was a house of correction for heresies, and William Kent, in *An Encyclopaedia of London*, wrote: '… in 1563 a number of non-conformists, arrested in the house of a goldsmith in the parish of St. Martin in the Fields, were taken there … Margaret Ward, in 1588, was hanged, drawn and quartered there for assisting the escape of William Watson, a priest who had been imprisoned in the "little ease" …'

Burglary
The act of breaking into a property by night.

Chance Medley
A self-defence killing in a halted physical encounter (obsolete).

Chantry
This was the tradition whereby rich citizens paid for a chapel in a church where priests would sing masses, to remember the souls of the dead. In 1547, as John Richardson notes in his *Local Historian's Encyclopaedia*, almost 2,400 chantries were suppressed.

Common Law
The unwritten old law of the land, supported and defined by group/court decisions. It stands opposed to equity, from the court of chancery.

Compter
These were prisons under the control of a sheriff. 'Sometimes they were in the sheriff's own house' (William Kent, *An Encyclopaedia of London*).

The compter in Wood Street later became the site of a police station, and Kent adds an entertaining fact: 'In 1628, Dr. Lambe, a man charged with certain evil and execrable arts called witchcraft, who is said to have supplied the Duke of Buckingham with love philtres … died here.'

Constable

There was a constable appointed for a court leet – manorial court – and also a constable as part of the parish's remit and responsibility. He had to take care of the watch and ward provision for community security, and was in charge of punishments ordered by the local court, such as stocks and pillory. From 1662 he could benefit from a local rate that would give him payments. Reading crime history through the ages, at any point before 1829 and the work of Sir Robert Peel, the historian will notice the presence of the hard-working and barely supported constables in almost every story.

Coverture

The working of law that in many ways eclipsed the wife in a marriage, depriving her of many rights we now see today as fundamental. However, with this situation came some privileges linked to ownership and rights under husbandry protection.

Equity

This was the court involved in additional and sometimes corrective work in relation to the common law. It would potentially deal with some kind of decision for a plaintiff who had appeared and been judged by the common law procedures and decisions.

Erastian

The line of thought and belief placing the church below the state in terms of authority. The origin of the word is from German thinker Thomas Lieber, whose surname was Grecianised as 'the lovely' – *Erastus.* The term 'erastian' can naturally be applied to the Church of England.

Felon/Felony

Originally, this was any capital crime committed with an intention of evil. In effect it is denotes a serious crime when related to the designated action in common law or in a statute.

Great Chain of Being

The medieval and renaissance concept of the whole of divine and human creation being a divine structure of harmony and hierarchy. In the classic work on this, E.M.W. Tillyard's book, *The Elizabethan World Picture*, the author quotes this passage by Nemesius, about man's place in the great scheme of creation, written in the fourth century:

> No eloquence may worthily publish forth the manifold pre-eminences and advantages which are bestowed on this creature [man]. He passeth over the vast seas; he rangeth about the wide heavens by his contemplation and conceives the motions and magnitude of the stars … He is learned in every science and skilful in artificial workings … He talketh with angels yea with God himself. He hath all the creatures within his dominion.

Habeas Corpus

A writ to demand an appearance of a said person before court and justices. Its importance is well stated by John B. Saunders in his dictionary of law: 'This is the most celebrated writ in the English law, being the great remedy which that law has provided for the violation of personal liberty.'

Hundred

John Richardson neatly explains the possibilities of the origin of this: 'A division of a shire especially important in Saxon and Norman times. There are several theories still held as to its origin. One is that it consisted of a hundred families, or ten tithings. Another is that it was an amount which contained 100 geld hides.' (Geld – skinned, bare) (*The Local Historian's Encyclopaedia*).

Indictment

The written statement defining the actual criminal charge applied to the offender.

Lollardy

The name given to the early reformers and people who espoused the ideas on religion put forward by John Wycliffe. Ebenezer Brewer gives a note on the origin: '… the name is from the Middle Dutch *lollaerd*, a mutterer, one who mumbles over prayers and hymns'. (*Dictionary of Phrase and Fable*).

Mutability

Literally, the condition of change or constant instability of nature and created material. In Edmund Spenser's *Faerie Queene* folio edition of 1609, two cantos describe the opposition of the father of the gods, Jove against the titaness Mutabilitie. The result is an account of the harmony on God's divine creation – the structure of the great chain of being.

Poursuivant

This refers mainly to a queen's or king's messenger. Strictly, the reference is to the official messengers who worked by travelling with royal documents or documents of state, but in crime reports through the ages, they took part in work against crime and in support of the magistrates and other regional persons in power.

Privateer

This is a vessel that has a commission to take control of or rob another vessel. Hence the letter of marque or reprisal used in authorised piracy.

Process

Principally, this refers to the use of a writ, directing the appearance of a defendant in a legal action.

Quarter Sessions (Court)

The Quarter Sessions courts were always the workhorse of the criminal justice system throughout British history. They began in 1351, and they handled every kind of offence and local tribulation that came their way. They were the domain of the justices of the peace (magistrates) and met, as the name suggests, four times a year. Before the justices came concerns relating to drunkenness, pub brawls, arguments over land, nuisances on the highway, problems with beggars, licensing of beer houses, provision of constables, maintenance of bridges and other affairs, the topics changing as the years passed and society had new laws and fresh social problems. All the justices of the county generally sat on the bench at Quarter Sessions.

Recognizance

A written statement, recording a person's words given to a magistrate, binding him or her to a court appearance, or to pay a debt etc., as directed. Often, these were statements by neighbours of accused, stating actions or things seen, relevant to a case under scrutiny.

Star Chamber (Court)

This old court was redefined under Henry VII in 1487 and had no jury, but was run by Privy Council members and judges, and dealt largely with major crimes such as riot, misbehaviour of those in office etc. Common Law judges were part of this. Abolished in 1640.

Tithing

In Saxon times, every male over the age of 12 had to be one of a group of men known as a tithing: this was a self-protective body of people accepting a role of security and support.

Treason Act (1351)

This Act has these acts considered then as treasonable:

> When a man compasses or imagines the death of our lord the king, of our lady his queen, or of their oldest son and heir.
>
> If a man do levy war against our lord the king in his realm.
>
> If a man do violate the king's companion, or the king's eldest daughter, or the wife of the king's eldest son and heir.
>
> If a man be adherent to the king's enemies, giving to them aid and comfort …
>
> If a man counterfeit the king's money, and if a man bring false money into the realm …
>
> If a man counterfeit the king's great or privy seal.
>
> If a man slay the chancellor, treasurer of the one bench or the other.

Writ

This is a command for an action to be taken in conjunction with some process in motion in the legal process. In crime history, various writs were used to have accused or witnesses appear in specific courts in order to facilitate the process of interrogation.

Acknowledgements

I would like to thank John B. Saunders and his law dictionary for help with the intricacies of legal language. In discussion, thanks go to Stuart Gibbon, Kate Walker and Andy Wade. Also, I owe thanks to staff at the University of Hull library, where my first researches into crime history began. Various online blogs and related material have been very helpful, and where I have not been able to give names, I can now give my thanks for some unusual reflections on interesting sources.

I also have to thank the bookseller Marie Elmer of Clifford Elmer Books, as from her catalogues I have used some of the black and white illustrations used here. Several other illustrations are from the Victorian journal series, *Old Yorkshire*, and these are itemised in the Bibliography.

Bibliography and Sources

Books Cited

Note: ***The Newgate Calendar:*** this rich source of criminal tales originated in *The Malefactor's Register or New Newgate and Tyburn Calendar,* published at the close of the eighteenth century. I have referenced, therefore, editions of the publication because different editorial series have seen print.

Abbott, Geoffrey, *Execution* (Summersdale, 2005)

Ackroyd, Peter, *Shakespeare, the Biography* (Vintage Books, 2005)

Anon., *A Rehearsal Both Strong and True, of Heinous and Horrible Acts Committed by Elizabeth Stile, Alias Rockingham* (for Edward White, 1579)

Archibald, Elizabeth P., *Ask the Past* (Vintage, 2015)

Ashton, John, *Chapbooks of the Eighteenth Century* (Skoob Books, no date)

Birkett, Sir Norman (Ed.), *The Newgate Calendar* (The Folio Society, 1951)

Briggs, Katharine M., *British Folk Tales: A Sampler* (Paladin, 1978)

Chesterton, G.K., *Essays and Poems* (Penguin, 1958)

Costin, W.C. and Watson, J. Steven (Eds.), *The Law and Working of the Constitution Documents 1660–1914*, Vol. 1, 1660–1783 (A. & C. Black, 1952)

Cronin, Vincent, *The Flowering of the Renaissance* (Collins/Fontana, 1969)

D'Cruze, Shani, Walklate, Sandra, and Pegg, Samantha, *Murder* (Willan, 2006)

Earle, Peter, *Sailors: English Merchant Seamen 1650–1775* (Methuen, 1998)

Elton, G.R., *Star Chamber Stories* (Methuen, 1958)

Fowles, John, *The French Lieutenant's Woman* (Pan Books, 1969)

Goodman, Ruth, *How to Behave Badly in Renaissance Britain* (Michael O'Mara, 2020)

Halliday, Paul D., *Habeas Corpus: From England and to Empire* (Harvard University Press, 2010)

Hibbert, Christopher, *The Roots of Evil* (Sutton, 2003)

Hirst, Joseph H., *The Blockhouses of Kingston-Upon-Hull and Who Went There* (A. Brown and Sons, 1913)

Howard, John, *The State of the Prisons* (Dent, 1929)

Irving, Ronald, *The Law Is an Ass* (Duckworth, 1999)

Jones, Terry, *Medieval Lives* (BBC Books, 2004)

Jusserand, J.J., *English Wayfaring Life in the Middle Ages* (T. Fisher Unwin, 1899)

Kee, Robert, *The Most Distressful Country: The Green Flag*, Vol. 1 (Penguin Books, 1989)

Lucie-Smith, Edward (Ed.), *The Penguin Book of Elizabethan Verse* (Penguin, 1965)

Machiavelli, Niccolo, *The Prince* (Penguin, 2011)

Maitland, F.W., *The Constitutional History of England* (Cambridge University Press, 1911)

McCall, Andrew, *The Medieval Underworld* (Sutton, 2004)

Morton, H.V., *In Search of Ireland* (Methuen, 1930)

Newby, Eric, *Slowly Down the Ganges* (Pan, 1983)

Nicholl, Charles, *The Reckoning* (Jonathan Cape, 1992)

Plowden, Alison, *Danger to Elizabeth* (Sutton Publishing, 2000)

Seddon, Peter, *The Law's Strangest Cases* (Robson Books, 1988)

Sharpe, J.A., *Witchcraft in Seventeeth-Century Yorkshire: Accusations and Counter Measures* (Borthwick Paper No. 81, 1992)

Sharpe, James (J.A.), *Witchcraft in Early Modern England* (Longman, 2001)

Stow, John, *A Survey of London Written in the Year 1598* (Sutton Publishing, 2009)

Taylor, Rev. R.V., *Yorkshire Anecdotes* (Whittaker & Co., 1873)

Thomas, Donald (Ed.), *State Trials Vol. 2 The Public Conscience* (Routledge and Kegan Paul, 1972)

Thompson, E.P., *Customs in Common* (Penguin, 1991)

Tillyard, E.M.W., *The Elizabethan World Picture* (Pimlico, 1998)

Tripp, H. Alker, *Suffolk Sea-Borders* (John Lane, The Bodley Head, 1926)

Turner, J. Horsfall, *Yorkshire Notes and Queries* (T. Harrison, 1890)

Wheeler-Holohan, V., *The History of the King's Messengers* (Grayson & Grayson, 1935)

Wiggins, Martin (Ed.), *A Woman Killed With Kindness and Other Domestic Plays* (OUP, 2008)

Wilkinson, Frederick, *Those Entrusted With Arms* (Royal Armouries, 2002)

Younghusband, Sir George, *The Tower of London* (Herbert Jenkins, 1924)

Reference Works

Anon., *Everyman's Encyclopaedia* (Readers Union, 1952)

Anon., *Jack's Reference Book* (Thomas Nelson, no date, *c.*1930)

Anon., *John Gregg and His Family of Robbers and Murderers*, chapbook, en.wikisource.org/wiki/*The History of John Gregg and His Family of Robbers* (Glasgow, 1789)

Beadle, Jeremy and Harrison, Ian, *Firsts, Lasts & Onlys: Crime* (Robson Books, 2007)

Baker, J.H., *An Introduction to English Legal History* (Butterworths, 2002)

Bellamy, J.G., *The Law of Treason in England in the Later Middle Ages* (Cambridge University Press, 1970)

Block, Brian P. and Hostettler, John, *Famous Cases: Nine Trials That Changed the Law* (Waterside Press, 2002)
Cannon, John, *Oxford Dictionary of British History* (OUP, 2001)
Carr-Gomm, Philip and Heygate, Richard, *The Book of English Magic* (Hodder & Stoughton, 2014)
Chambers, Robert, *Traditions of Edinburgh* (W. & R. Chambers, 1931)
Coss, P., *The Lady in Medieval England, 1000–1500* (Tempus, 1998)
Cowie, L.W., *The Wordsworth Dictionary of British Social History* (Wordsworth, 1973)
Cyriax, Oliver, *The Penguin Encyclopaedia of Crime* (Penguin, 1993)
Davies, Owen, *Grimoires: A History of Magic Books* (Oxford University Press, 2009)
Dobson, Mary, *Murderous Contagion: A Human History of Disease* (Quercus, 2007)
Drabble, Margaret, *The Oxford Companion to English Literature* (Oxford University Press, 1987)
Friar, Stephen, *The Sutton Companion to Local History* (Sutton, 2001)
Hackwood, Frederick W., *Inns, Ales and Drinking Customs of Old England* (Bracken Books, 1985)
Herber, Mark, *Legal London: A Pictorial History* (Phillimore, 1999)
Kent, William, *An Encyclopaedia of London* (Dent, 1951)
Linnane, Fergus, *The Encyclopaedia of London Crime and Vice* (Sutton Publishing, 2003)
Morris, Norval & Rothman, David J., *The Oxford History of the Prison* (Oxford University Press, 1998)
National Trust, *Croft Castle and Parkland*, www.nationaltrust.org.uk
Paley, Ruth and Fowler, Simon, *Family Skeletons* (The National Archives, 2005)
Partridge, Colonel S.G., *Prisoner's Progress* (Hutchinson & Co., undated)
Peacock, A.J. (Ed.), *Essays in York History* (York History, undated)
Rede, Leman, *York Castle* (J. Saunders, 1829)
Richardson, John, *The Local Historian's Encyclopaedia* (Historical Publications, 1974)

Robinson, Tony, *The Worst Jobs in History: A Vivid and Disgusting Alternative History of Britain* (Boxtree, 2004)

Saul, Nigel, *A Companion to Medieval England 1066–1485* (Tempus, 2005)

Saunders, John B. (Ed.), *Mozley and Whiteley's Law Dictionary* (Butterworths, 1977)

Schama, Simon, *A History of Britain: At the Edge of the World?* (BBC, 2000)

Scott, Sir Harold (Ed.), *The Concise Encyclopaedia of Crime and Criminals* (Andre Deutsch, 1951)

Seddon, Peter, *The Law's Strangest Cases* (Robson Books, 2005)

Stretton, Tim, *Women Waging War in Elizabethan England* (Cambridge University Press, 1998)

Vandome, Nick, *Crimes and Criminals* (Chambers, 1992)

Journals, Essays and Press

Brooks, F.W., 'Yorkshire and the Star Chamber', The East Yorkshire Local History Society, 1954

Brown, Bernard J., 'The Demise of Chance Medley and the Recognition of Provocation As a Defence to Murder in English Law', *American Journal of Legal History,* Vol. 7, p.210

Campbell, Ruth, 'Sentence of Death by Burning for Women', *Journal of Legal History*

Canning, Ruth, Review of Steven Ellis, *Ireland's English Pale* in *History Ireland*

Flannery, Mary C., 'The Case for the Defence', *Times Literary Supplement*, 21 October 2022, p.18

Hordern, John, 'The Renaissance Emblem Book' in *Antiquarian Book Monthly*, Vol. VIII, No. 1, Issue 81, January 1981, pp.10–13

Kane, Stuart A., 'Wives with Knives: Early Modern Murder Ballads and the Transgressive Commodity', *Criticism*, Winter 1996, Vol. XXXVIII, No. 2, pp.219–237

Kleineke, Hans, 'Richard III and the Origins of the Court of Requests', Biblio://richardiii.net>uploads>2021/08

Klerman, Daniel, 'Review of Women Waging War in Elizabethan England' at www.cambridge.org./core

Malcolm-Davies, Dr Jane, 'Codpieces, Caps and Kirtles: Secrets of Tudor Fashion' in *Tudor Life* (BBD History Extra, 2025), pp.69–73

Salingar, L.G., 'Tourneur and the Tragedy of Revenge', in Ford, Boris (Ed.), *The Pelican Guide to English Literature: The Age of Shakespeare* (Penguin, 1969), pp.334–354

Shepard, Alexandra, 'Worthless Witnesses? Marginal Voices and Women's Legal Agency in Early Modern England', *Journal of British Studies 58*, October 2019, pp.717–734

Sidsworth, Tim and Penna, Dominic, 'Judge: Right to Offend is part of Free Speech', *The Daily Telegraph*, 11 September 2025, p.4

Smith, William, 'The Ducking Stool at Morley', *Old Yorkshire* (Longmans Green, 1881), pp.127–128

Stone, Lawrence, 'Interpersonal Violence in English Society 1300–1980', *Past and Present,* No. 101, November 1983, pp.22–33

Stoyle, Mark, 'Tudor Rebellion' in *Tudor Life* (BBC HistoryExtra, 2025), pp.90–95

Sumption, Jonathan, 'Little England, Big France', review of Michael Livingston's *The Two Hundred Years War* (*Times Literary Supplement*, 31 October 2025, p.33

Taylor, R.V., 'Yorkshire Clergy Sufferings', *Old Yorkshire* (Longmans Green, 1881), pp.139–143

The Historical Journal, No. 19, Vol. 2, pp.501–509

Van der Slice, Austin, 'Elizabethan Houses of Correction', *American Institute of Criminology*, 45 (1936–37), pp.45–67

Weiss, Michael, 'A Power in the North? The Percies in the Fifteenth Century', www.cambridge.org/stable/2638574

Wheater, William, 'Witches and Wizards', *Old Yorkshire* (Longmans Green, 1883), pp.165–271

Wrigglesworth, Edmund, 'Sufferings of the Roman Catholics', *Old Yorkshire* (Longmans Green, 1881), pp.139–141

Internet Sources

www.bristol.ac.uk >news

British History Online: 169 Dowman v Faulcon see https://british-history.ac.uk

History of England podcast feed *The Six Articles 1539*/Things that made England podcast,

https://archive.org > statepapersmry01greauoft_djvu

McSheffrey, Dr Shannon, *Sanctuary Seekers in England, 1394–1557*, https://sanctuaryseekers.ca

Payling, Dr Simon, 'The Barbarity of the Medieval Criminal Law: Petty Treason and the Murders of Sir Thomas Murdak and John Cotell' at *The History of the British Parliament*, www.parliamentUK/*about-living-heritage*

www.ebsco.com >research starters > history. (For material on the death of Thomas Cranmer, this offers a vivid account of his end.

Other Sources

Agee, Susan, *The Court of Star Chamber*, Honours thesis, 232 University of Richmond, 1969

Anon., 'Relations with that Woman? No', *The Times*, 29 September 1925, p.16

Arnold, Catherine, 'Ben Jonson's Murder Charge' in *London Historians'* Blog: https://londonhistorians.wordpress.com/2018/11/21/ben-jonsons-murder-charge

The High Sheriff of Oxfordshire's Annual Law Lecture Given by Lord Wilson on 9 October 2012 at https://supremecourt.uk>speeches

Flannigan, Laura, *Justice in the Court of Requests 1483–1538,* PhD thesis, June 2020, University of Cambridge

'Gloucester Gaols, Prisons & Bridewells', Gloucestershire Archives

Index